WITCH

WOMAN IN TOTAL CONTROL OF HERSELF

The Ultimate Guide to Manifest Money, Love and Success!

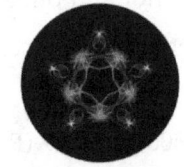

By Karen Stevens

WITCH

By Karen Stevens

First Edition 2020

Copyright © 2020 Karen Stevens

All rights reserved. No part of this publication may be reproduced, stored in a retrieval system, or transmitted in any form or by any means, electronic, mechanical, photocopying, recording or otherwise, without the prior written permission from both the copyright owner and publisher.

Disclaimer

All the information, techniques, skills, and concepts contained within this publication are of the nature of general comment only and are not in any way recommended as individual advice. The intent is to offer a variety of information to provide a wider range of choices now and in the future, recognising that we all have widely diverse circumstances and viewpoints. Should any reader choose to make use of the information contained herein, this is their decision and the author and publishers do not assume any responsibilities whatsoever under any condition or circumstances.

ISBN: 9780648995807 (Paperback)

For more information about the author, Karen Stevens, or for additional trainings, speaking engagements, or media enquiries, please visit:
www.karenstevens.com.au

IT'S TIME TO CELEBRATE!

Download Your Free Quantum Leap Activation

As a way of saying thank you for purchasing a copy of my book, I'm gifting you a free Activation Download that is exclusive to readers of WITCH.

Quantum Leap into Unconditional Love
Clear your energy and upgrade your frequency
Instantly shift into a deeper connection within
Open to receive all the Universe has to offer - Abundance, Joy, Freedom and Peace.

https://karenstevenswitch.lpages.co/witch-free-gift

CONNECT WITH KAREN STEVENS AT:

www.karenstevens.com.au
facebook.com/karen.528hz.stevens
instagram.com/___karenstevens___/
www.linktr.ee/karenstevensW.I.T.C.H
email: karen@karenstevens.com.au

This book is dedicated to all women.
May we rise and thrive together and create Magick along the way!

To my beautiful children, Eloise and James, who infused the breath of life within me, connecting me to the infinite peace and joy of unconditional love.
I love the amazing humans that you are.
Love you to infinity and beyond,
Mum xo

A Special Thank You

A very special thank you to my book coach and mentor, Emma Hamlin.

You my darling, are the ultimate Change maker and I am truly blessed to know you and love you. Thank you for your support and invaluable guidance. Forever grateful for you xx

Thank You

I wanted to take this opportunity to thank the many mentors, spiritual teachers and guides I have had over my lifetimes, without your love and advice I wouldn't be penning this book.

To every author of every book I have ever read, to every transmission I have listened to, every meditation I have experienced and every download I have received that has in some way shaped who I am today – I say thank you.

And to The Creator of All That Is – thank you for the journey.

Contents

Introduction 1

Chapter 1: My Journey. The Path From Past To Present W.I.T.C.H And Owning It! 5

Chapter 2: Why Is There So Much Negativity Around The Word "Witch"? 15

Chapter 3: How Do I Connect To My Inner W.I.T.C.H? 27

Chapter 4: Start With Love For Love Is The Beginning And The End. 67

Chapter 5: What Exactly Do I Want? 81

Chapter 6: Declutter Your Mind. Clearing Limiting Beliefs And Self-Sabotage. 103

Chapter 7: Curses, Psychic Attacks And Karma 135

Chapter 8: Setting Powerful Intentions 151

Chapter 9: Confused About Manifesting? 163

Chapter 10: Daily Practice. It Is All In The Cultivation. 171

Chapter 11: Call In Love And Your Divine Soulmate Connections. 195

Chapter 12: Calling In Money, Wealth, And Abundance 219

Chapter 13: Improving Your Health. 237

Chapter 14: Want To Delve Deeper Into The W.I.T.C.H Shift And How You Can Help Other Women Activate Their Magick? 259

Chapter 15: Your Magic Toolbox.   Use This Toolbox Jam Packed With All The Invocations And Extra Bonuses. 265

Afterword 335

INTRODUCTION

What an amazing journey writing this book has been.

You see before writing this book, I was playing it safe. I was not embracing all that I am.

Even though I considered myself to be a very powerful healer; having helped many other women to heal their lives, and an equally resilient woman, having overcome so much trauma in my own life; nothing could have prepared me for the completeness of the surrendering I would experience by sharing my absolute truth in its purest form.

I welcome you into my world of magic, miracles and being limitless. The world of the W.I.T.C.H (Woman in Total Control of Herself).

Each chapter in this book will lead you into surrendering all that is blocking your path to manifesting the life you dream about. Every incantation, invocation, activation and spell is designed specifically to ignite that spark in you, to awaken the power of your Magick and to align your frequency gracefully yet powerfully with your Divine birthright of Abundance.

In this book I genuinely share with you my life's work so you too may embrace all that you are.

Begin each chapter with an open mind and an open heart, surrender to the guidance that is before you and you will receive what you need. Remain open to new ideas, have patience, and trust this process; it will open you to unlimited possibilities, activate your Magick and ignite your potential to shine brighter than ever.

My intention is for this book to be a catalyst in raising the collective consciousness, ending the generations of persecution of women and myths around the powerful gift of Magick.

It is time for women to rise and be revered once more for the wisdom that is bestowed within our very DNA. It is time for you to step into being a WITCH.

CHOOSE YOU

YOU ARE BEING ASKED TO CHOOSE TO DO WHAT YOU LOVE.

LET GO OF THE EXPECTATIONS AND ALLOW YOURSELF TO FOLLOW YOUR PASSIONS.

DOING WHAT YOU LOVE CREATES MORE HAPPINESS AND JOY.

AFFIRMATION:

I CHOOSE TO DO WHAT I LOVE.

CHAPTER 1

My journey. The path from past to present W.I.T.C.H and owning it!

FROM HUMBLE BEGINNINGS

It was October 15, 1970 and the West Gate Bridge in Melbourne, Australia collapses killing 35 men, and it was the day I made my entrance into this world.

Born into the trauma of this calamity, it is not surprising that my life would follow this trajectory for many, many years to follow.

This lifetime for me has not been an easy ride, that is safe to say, growing up in an abusive home with a narcissistic alcoholic mother, I never ever felt safe, wanted, or loved. Her physical and emotional abuse had devastating effects on the empath I am. Sexually abused by several family members served to only confuse me further about my place in this world.

I felt things deeply. So much more deeply than others. I could sense energy, feelings, and thoughts, communicate with spirit, predict things, see the future; and the volatile nature of my childhood only served to seriously impact the way in which I would experience this life.

Bullied throughout school, I knew I was different. I felt it. So, at 15, when one boy pursued me relentlessly, I gave in and let my protective wall down. I saw this as an opportunity to escape the abuse of my mother, but it only led me on a more soul-destroying path.

18 years of emotional, physical, sexual abuse and slavery were to follow with him, and the daily beatings and heartache I felt almost completely shut down my gifts until I finally broke free with the help of a work colleague.

I was broken, damaged, alone, and frightened. This world was not what I expected.

I repeated the cycle of violence twice more before a near death experience brought me rushing back into my body with the reminder that I had so much more to do here on this planet.

I was 43 years old. I had two children under 8 and was so tired of living, but something inside me was rising. I could feel it. I had been so disconnected for so long, just so that I could survive this world, but this near-death experience had flicked the switch.

My gifts began to flow back in, and I could "feel" so much more, the visions and predictions came thick and fast. I started to follow my instinct, my intuition; and the more I did the more I aligned I became with my true self, that bright spark that I thought had been extinguished long ago.

The journey back to self was a tough one, as I was often challenged to return to the addiction of abuse; after all, it was all I knew; all I had experienced.

My children kept me focused, every time I felt myself waiver, I would look at their beautiful faces and into their innocent eyes and know that I must change this pattern for them. I must stand in my power and own my differences and help other women to do the same.

It took years of mastery; mastering my emotions and my empathic nature, my sensitivities and of learning how to use these sensitivities to benefit myself and others.

As an empath, I would learn, is one of the greatest gifts, and one that is the most challenging to master. The heightened senses mean that an empath will feel the emotion at its very core, magnified and unfiltered. This can be very overwhelming and takes practice and patience to master, not unlike the mastery the monk or Sensei learns. It is a spiritual practice and a practice of the mind, where one meets the other and forms an alliance. A connection. An understanding.

As I learned and healed my life of the trauma, I took other women on that journey with me, into their power, helping them to fully embrace every part of themselves; building resilience, courage, confidence, and connection so they could master self-love.

They say we teach what we most need to learn, and for me, this was absolutely true.

As a child not feeling loved, safe, or valued, this was one of my biggest lessons and something I needed to master if I were to assist others to truly embrace all that they are.

The feeling of unconditional love for self is such a freeing and amazing experience. To know and feel on every level that you need for nothing as it all resides within. And this was the key for me.

For years I worked closely with women, domestic violence victims, victims of abuse, those women that had suffered severe trauma to assist them to release that trauma from their DNA and reconnect to their own inner power. Using my intuition and my gifts I was able to help them create lives full of joy, contentment, passion and unshakeable self-love, just as I had been able to do for myself.

I felt so blessed and knew I was following my purpose when I was recognized and awarded for my work in inspiring other women, and for being a catalyst for change. A Changemaker.

It had been a wild ride, but nothing could have prepared me for the next stage of my journey.

Fully, completely stepping into all that I am. Total recognition of my souls' unique Divine purpose.

Working with Quantum energy was so very exciting to me, and as I was about to discover it was because I was unknowingly tapping into this Ancestral Magick that was inside of me all along.

My inner WITCH.

THE MOMENT OF TRUTH

It all began as I sat in that chair, deep in a past life regression, I felt my soul traveling back in time. I began to hurtle towards a time long, long ago.

Sitting atop a hill of sorts, with a valley below, overlooking a small village I watch as people of all ages take the journey from the valley.

They are walking in single file up a narrow path etched into the side of the hill. The ground looks damp and a mist fills parts of the valley below. The air is crisp and the smell of the fire burning in a circle in front of me stings my nostrils and my eyes tear up.

As I view the scene I am in, I can see myself; a woman nearing seventy, with long grey hair that is wild and wiry. I look to my left and I see another woman and feel surprised as she looks just like me!

It is my identical twin sister with the same wild hair. She smiles at me; and as I look into her large soulful eyes, I recognize her, and her eyes begin to tell me the story of our lives together as I feel drawn into them like a mirror to my soul.

I am instantly transported into my Akashic Records. The 11th century.

Sitting cross legged in front of the fire we chant as we call in the Great Spirit, the Creator of All.

A young girl approaches being ushered by her mother. The mother's weary face is a tell-tale sign that they have been traveling for a long time to get here. The girl, according to her mother, has never spoken, and her mother desperately wants her to be able to speak, and to hear her daughter's voice.

I place my hand on the girl's forehead and begin to see the story of her life playing out in my own mind. I am shown through her generational lines, her past lives, all the records held within her body's energy systems and her DNA; pinpointing the moment that robbed this little girl of her voice.

Laying the little girl down, I place Tigers Eye and Black Tourmaline along the 12 activation points, and I begin a spell to cast out the curse and restore this girl's voice. I open the spell book, my sister burning small bags of herbs over the circle of fire as I recite the spell to release the curse.

The little girl shudders as the curse is broken. I hand the girl a cup of powerful medicinal herbs, and she takes a sip, then, miraculously utters her first sound, and then another and another. Tears of joy flow down her mother's cheeks and the little girl has a smile as bright as the sun.

It appears that we are well known "witches" and revered throughout England and through my sister's eyes I can see the hundreds of people that make the journey to be healed of their ailments.

We hand out tinctures and potions, work spells, cast out evil spirits and heal the sick, releasing them from suffering.

I am shown that this is an ancient wisdom that was bestowed upon our bloodlines. A powerful mix of shamanism, witchcraft, ancient medicines, psychic intuitions, quantum energy and the secrets of the Universe.

Suddenly the scene changes and I am taken to the darkness of night. I am awoken as an army of men tie my sister and I both, in ropes, and carry us down the hill into the valley. We are slumped over the back of a horse and taken in silence on a very long journey. In what seems to be a day or two, we arrive at a castle; a chateau that is surrounded by rivers and valleys.

It is William the Conqueror who has ordered for our capture. He has heard of our "witchcraft" and wants us to assist him in securing the throne. In this period, witchcraft was highly praised and practiced.

My sister and I refuse as we will not use our witchcraft for tyranny, and we are held and tortured for what feels likes weeks as we continue to be "strongly encouraged" to obey.

The 11th century was a time of great conflict and saw the end of the Viking Age and the subsequent crowning of William The Conqueror.

I had been living through both the 10th and 11th century and had witnessed much change, not unlike my current incarnation, living in both the 20th and 21st century and the rapid evolution of technology and the internet.

William finally orders our death as we continue to refuse to comply to his demands and we are promptly executed with a sword through the abdomen.

As I feel the pain and burn of the sword as it pushes through my abdomen and exits through my spine, I look over and see the life force energy leaving my sister's body as she too is executed.

As I watch this scene play out, I realize that our secrets of Magick and our bloodlines have ended right there in that moment; no further surviving kin to pass on this wisdom to.

As I watch myself die, I begin to feel myself being pulled upwards.

I am on another planet! I feel at home. So peaceful. And I am receiving the information that this IS my home. This is Sirius.

Right here in this past life regression I am being shown my full life purpose, all laid out in front of me on a virtual screen. The full embodiment of my true essence; the Ancestral Magick that lives within my DNA, the acceptance of my innate spiritual gifts and healing abilities.

I am a star seed, a cosmic activation portal, and I am here to assist in making change in this world, to help shift the consciousness of the planet.

I am being shown the power and purity of my Magick; and the message is crystal clear.

To reignite the Magick that runs throughout my ancestry and to teach women to activate the power of Magick that also resides within them. To activate their inner W.I.T.C.H.

As my senses come back into the room and I open my eyes, the sheer enormity of what I just witnessed dawns on me.

Now is the time I must fully step into that power. I must own my Magick, and every one of my gifts.

I must claim my mission.

Releasing not only my own persecution but the persecution of all women that has been stored within our DNA and ancestry for hundreds upon hundreds of years. This is about challenging and changing the negative perceptions and paradigms around witches and witchcraft; to welcome in the new generation of wise women who are not afraid to speak their truth and to use their knowledge and gifts for the wellbeing and freedom of humanity. The new quantum W.I.T.C.H.

CHANCE MEETING OR DESTINY IN PLAY?

I have been reunited with that twin sister. Our souls meeting 7 years ago. Although we are not related in this lifetime, the bond we share in indisputable.

She was the missing puzzle piece that would bring me closer to my true Divine purpose. I now understand why I was blessed with the opportunity to assist her on her own healing journey, and why it was imperative that I help her to reclaim her spiritual gifts in this lifetime. It was all part of a deeper activation within me, to fully stepping up into my full W.I.T.C.H power.

This moment in time is an important one and I am so honoured to be able to share this with you in this book, helping you to remember who you truly are; beyond the external influences in your life, to assist you to tap into the deep reservoir that is your authentic self. The W.I.T.C.H within.

It is a time for celebration in the world, a time of women rising.

CHOOSE YOU

YOU ARE BEING ASKED TO CHOOSE TO LET GO OF ALL JUDGEMENT,

OF YOURSELF AND OF OTHERS TO ALLOW THE FREEDOM TO EXPRESS YOUR TRUE,

AUTHENTIC SELF.

AFFIRMATION:

I CHOOSE TO LET GO OF ALL JUDGEMENT.

CHAPTER 2

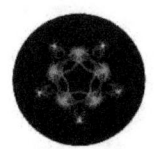

Why is there so much negativity around the word "witch"?

In this chapter I want to dispel the negativity around the word *witch*.

Witches were wise women. Women that could communicate with spirit, were connected to the Universe, to Mother Nature and to ALL of existence. They understood herbal medicines, were completely connected to their own intuition, and connected with the Divine; they were held in the highest of esteem because they could create miracles in everyday life. A complete reflection of Mother Earth - The ultimate creators of life.

So, to truly demystify *witchcraft*, we first need to look at the etymology of the word *witch* itself.

Understanding how the word evolved and morphed into what we know today will give you a better understanding of why *witches* have been perceived as "evil" and "dark" and have been persecuted for hundreds of years.

As I deeply dived into this, I should note that searching the Oxford English Dictionary, I learned that the word *witch* is "of uncertain origin".

The reason for this is simply because *witch* has too many potential genealogies.

One of the most popular etymologies for *witch* is that it is related to the English words wit, wise, and wisdom. For me personally, these make a lot of sense considering the ancient wisdom that runs in our DNA and our ancestry.

There are other claims that *witch* is adopted from the root meaning to be "holy" or "sacred", or from a set of Germanic words that indicate a magical practice related to divination.

Other suggestions include the meanings "to bend" referring to a *witch's* ability to bend reality, the Indo-European meaning to "be strong, be lively", or in the Sanskrit "strength and speed".

Appearing again in Old English verbs *wacian* "to be awake" or "to watch, to stay awake".

The connotation of the *witch* as the "watcher" or "wakeful one" completely aligns with me, as women all over the world awaken to their innate gifts and wisdom.

In the earliest centuries of human civilization, women who served the goddesses were *witches*. They were revered throughout their communities.

In Asia, Egypt and Turkey, ancient civilizations not only worshiped powerful female deities, but it was most often the women who practiced the holiest of rituals. Trained in these sacred arts, these wise women may have been some of the earliest manifestations of what we now acknowledge as the *witch*.

No matter the label, these wise women were positive influencers, leaders, and pillars of their societies. They made house calls, delivered, and blessed babies, cured ailments and illnesses, dealt with infertility and more.

Witches were revered.

So how did this once revered wise woman transform into the perception of the evil and malevolent witch portrayed in the 21st century?

It has been written that the shift in belief came long before the birth of Christ, when the Indo-Europeans expanded, bringing the consciousness into alignment with a warrior culture that worshipped male Gods of War, and this then dominated the once-revered female deities.

Others believe it was the Hebrews that labelled *witchcraft* as dangerous and banned its use, prohibiting it as a pagan practice.

It seems there are many, varied beliefs – all appearing to be rooted into fear at some level.

As I looked forward into the 12th century, I noted that they were wrought with fear during the plague that annihilated Europe; killing one in three people, and they attributed their misfortune to the Devil and his worshippers. This brought with it mass hysteria and a vehement fear of *witches*, thanks to Christianity. Christianity had certainly changed the beliefs of much of society, pairing *witches* with The Devil and all things evil.

The Catholic Church's Inquisition, established decades earlier, extended the efforts to seek out and punish the non-Catholic causes of the mass deaths, which included these "Devil worshipping" *witches*. In order to "save" the Church and its followers from the Devil, the Catholic Church produced a book, *Malleus Maleficarum* to assist *witch* hunters in diagnosing and punishing these so-called *witches*. These women who now found themselves in a male dominated society, were seen to be sexually vulnerable and therefore easy pray for the Devil, and must be "tamed".

At the time, *Malleus Maleficarum* was second only to the Bible in terms of popularity and the book would serve as a platform for devout *witch* hunters to act on and act out their prejudices for well over two hundred years!

Even though there had been other *witch* hunting books written before *Malleus Maleficarum*, the writers of this book: two Catholic Monks, was the first to associate a specific gender (female) with *witchcraft*, thus demonizing women and as such the beginning of the persecution of women throughout time.

As the 15th century came to an end, *witch* hunting hysteria had reached its peak in Europe. *Witch* hunts were ablaze across most of Europe and the worst affected were in France and Germany. During this time, the *witch* hunts were so severe that in some towns there were no women at all left – every woman accused of *witchcraft* and executed.

Thousands of women were arrested, examined, stripped, and searched and any "suspicious" birth mark, mole or wart could be enough to receive the death sentence.

Torture was common, as to be able to execute the accused, they required a confession. Torture involved the Church's use of thumb and leg screws , head clamps, even the iron maiden to extract the "truth", *"the confession"*, to be able to order the death of these women *"witches"*.

This period did not end until the beginning of the 18th century and it is estimated that over 60,000 (mainly women) in Europe were slaughtered as *"witches"*.

Many methods of execution were used, all violent: burning, hanging, guillotine, and drowning.

Burning was said to be favoured as it was considered a more painful way to die.

And as women today, these painful physical deaths, the trauma of betrayal, shame, inequality and sacrifice are etched into our DNA.

Many parts of the world partook in *"witch hunts"*. One of the most infamous is the 17th century Salem *witch* trials.

These trials spread rapidly and became a "hunting hysteria" involving 24 outlying villages. Jails were crowded with more than two hundred accused *witches* awaiting trial, 27 were found guilty and 19 of them killed. The trials met a swift and dramatic end when victims began pointing the finger at high-ranking figures within the community and leaders saw to it that the trials ceased immediately.

As you can see, Christianity played a major role in shaping the future of our societies. Women were named and shamed, and the female consciousness suppressed for hundreds of years.

The women generally targeted as *"witches"* were women that were thought to be "social outcasts"; beggars, the poor, slaves, widows, single mothers, or those women took part in affairs outside of marriage or sexual relations outside of wedlock.

This shaped society's perception of women in general; whence at one time women were celebrated and revered for their spiritual and innate gifts, their healing abilities and for the nourishment, kindness and compassion they offered, they now could not be trusted and had become the bearers of curses, evil, and misfortune. Christianity offered the notion that men were the rulers, and must have control of their women folk, for fear of them being seduced by the Devil himself.

This is all ties into a fear-based reality. As humans we tend to revert to a state of hysteria when major crises unfold. We panic buy, judge, blame and criticize one another. As we hit that fight or flight switch, we act completely irrationally in the face of what we believe to be danger.

The indoctrination of people en-masse into a false archetypal salvation model of the crucified Christ, reprogrammed our communities across the world into the fear and guilt-based belief system of martyrdom. Anyone who did not conform was outcast and damned, the Catholic Church fearmongering by stating that there is no salvation for those that do not accept their religion.

Most religions elevated the status of men over women, and had stricter sanctions against women, that required them to be submissive. The marked shift in roles of men and women was considerable and women were not permitted to connect with their power.

This was an immense deprivation for women, and thus begun the great suppression of women the world over.

The healers, the seers and the bringers of light no longer felt safe to express their truth and our world suffered immensely. We see that suffering today as the economy plunges, the sick continue to become sicker, violence and crime escalates, we self-medicate with drugs and alcohol, and mental health issues are at an all-time high.

The persecution of women has been ingrained in our DNA for centuries and it is time for women to break free from those chains that have kept us "submissive, good girls" who need to beg for love and forgiveness for our perceived sins.

Women are rising and we must lead the way once more, to activate our Divine gifts of knowledge and wisdom and to unapologetically speak our truth. The truth of the Universe. The Divine Truth.

We are here to heal this world and unite humanity.

WHAT EXACTLY IS WITCHCRAFT?

Witchcraft has certainly had a bad rap for many centuries now, and there are many beliefs around what *witchcraft* really is. Many still see *witchcraft* as something bad, evil, or sinister. Something to be feared.

But *witchcraft* is on the rise in our modern world. Many women practicing *witchcraft* do so in covens or circles. Many practice rituals passed down for generations, or practice Wicca, and some love crystals and the power of the moon.

Whatever your take on *witchcraft* is I want to dispel some myths around what I believe is the true mastery of *witchcraft*.

When we looked back through history, a *witch* was revered, a wise woman. She was a healer that tapped into the power of her divinity.

Put simply a *witch* is a woman in total control of herself.

A *witch* is aware of her own power and puts that power into action.

She is the epitome of the Divine feminine and the Divine masculine in alignment, without duality, in Loving Oneness. She knows who she is, and she shares the gift of herself with the world; unapologetically.

So, *witchcraft* therefore, is the practice of being in your power, using your inner Magick to manifest and create situations and experiences that bring pleasure, joy and abundance to your life using ancient wisdom, spells, words of power, and quantum energy manipulation in harmony with the Universal Laws.

MAGICK is the art of channelling and directing energy using the universal laws to bring to life the desired effect.

Every one of us has an inner W.I.T.C.H we can reconnect to and activate to fully awaken our power.

And this guide will assist you to connect with that part of you, that has been dormant, patiently waiting for this moment in time to be rediscovered.

Limitless opportunities are available to you once you step into and own this inner W.I.T.C.H as you create magic and miracles in your everyday life.

WHAT IS THE DIFFERENCE BETWEEN WHITE MAGIC AND BLACK MAGIC?

There are many thoughts around black and white magic, and there is a simple way to define them.

Firstly all Magick is powerful. All Magick can be used for positive or negative. As there is light there is also darkness. As above, so below. You get my point.

It is so important that your frame of mind and your intention is positive when connecting into the power of your Magick. That everything you do is for the best and highest of all involved and does not diminish another's free will.

This is why I teach my private clients to release the negative patterns and beliefs, thoughts and feelings before truly stepping up into their full power. This will be covered in chapters 6, 7 and 8 to assist you to release those negative elements and experiences in your own life.

Practicing Magick is a craft, hence the craft in *witchcraft*. It is a discipline that requires you to be a clear conduit, practicing cleansing rituals, ensuring you are at your clearest to connect with the purest Divine energy and not transfer any of your own negative thoughts or energy into your spells, incantations or commands. Rather like the Hippocratic Oath a Doctor takes, as *witches* we must also abide to the Laws of the Universe when creating our Magick.

Your intention is powerful when casting a spell or creating Magick. If your intentions are negative or malicious, you will create something that goes against Universal Laws, and against the free will and choice of others, and this will have a Negative Karmic effect for you.

BLACK MAGIC

Black magic has traditionally referred to the use of Magick for evil or selfish purposes, invoking spirits to produce beneficial outcomes for the practitioner. Hexes cast to inflict misfortune on others for example, are indeed very, very real. I will also cover what to do if you feel you have been cursed and how you can break that curse in Chapter 7.

WHITE MAGIC

White magic on the other hand is referred to the use of Magick for healing, pursuing the ethics of kindness and goodness. White magic parallels the primitive shamanistic efforts to achieve closeness with spiritual beings. It represents the purity of the will of the individual toward acquisition of glory and power for positive intention and action.

I prefer to use the terms light and dark Magick, or high and low Magick as a basis for discernment when looking at Magick and the power that it holds.

Check in with yourself and ask – is my intention high or low, light, or dark? If you are feeling low or depressed and not in the right frame of mind it is best to not practice at that time and seek assistance from a fellow healer or practitioner to shift your energy. If you remember to be mindful and check in on your intentions, the creation of the spell will be in alignment for your best and highest good and the good of all.

CHOOSE YOU

YOU ARE BEING ASKED NOW TO STEP UP AND EMBRACE YOUR DIVINE GIFTS AND TALENTS

IT IS TIME FOR YOU TO CHOOSE YOU.

SHARE YOUR EXPERIENCES AND UNIQUE QUALITIES. SHINE BRIGHT TO ENCOURAGE AND INSPIRE OTHERS.

AFFIRMATION:

I CHOOSE TO EMBRACE MY GIFTS AND TALENTS.

CHAPTER 3

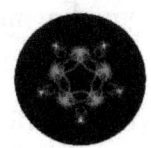

How do I connect to my inner W.I.T.C.H?

It is highly likely if you are reading this book, that the subject of Magick is of interest to you or intrigues you somewhat. The word *WITCH* sparks a curiosity within, and you feel a surge of excitement bubbling up.

You most likely have always felt different from others, like you do not quite fit in! You are sensitive to the world around you, an empath even, you may sense and feel pain and suffering; fear and hate, and you have an affinity with Mother Earth and nature.

You may feel, hear, or see spirit, have premonitions or hunches, Déjà vu, or experiences you cannot quite explain.

Welcome to the world of being magical. It is now time to fully express your own Magick in this world.

As a woman, you are the creator of life itself, birthing new life into this world.

This in itself is the most powerful and magical experience available; the ability to house another soul within your body, within you energy field, to nourish and nurture this soul until the moment they are ready to enter this world.

You are the ultimate guide from the moment of conception. Loving, nourishing, nurturing, and protecting this soul with every fibre of your being and strengthening their physical and spiritual immune systems.

You are to be revered. You are a Goddess, the Goddess of life itself.

"May you awaken to the bliss of the Divine Feminine within you. May her creative and infinite power remind you of who you truly are. The blending of the Divine male and Divine female energies in perfect harmony, allowing the sacred love and grace of the Goddess within your heart".

Understanding the magnitude of power that exists within you is the starting point to connecting to your inner W.I.T.C.H. – Woman in total control (connection) with herself.

The first most important thing is to understand that everything is energy. Science has now proven what many ancient practices have known all along.

Everything is energy, the Law of Vibration. When we look at this scientifically, when we go down to the smallest level (sub-atomic), matter is not visible, only pure energy - the Unified Field or The Matrix. Everything is connected to everything else. Nothing rests, it is constantly moving. The sea, the sky, the trees, and animals, you and me and the world around us. Everything comes from the same source of energy and returns to it. Everything is one.

Our thoughts and feelings are energy too, so everything we think and feel has an influence on everything and everyone on this planet – The

Collective Consciousness. This is how we create our own reality, because energy can penetrate matter.

Connect. Everything is energy, everything is one, and everything is possible.

QUANTUM MAGICK

You might by now be asking yourself the question: What is Quantum Magick?

When we look at Quantum mechanics, reality is described by waves defining the probabilities of different outcomes from the same interactions. These waves manifest as what we have been taught to call matter, energy, particles, or waves when observed.

As we possess a mixed blend of all three states of matter, according to Quantum Physics, we are also made up of these energy "quanta" (packs). These energy packs are also on a constant spin and move, radiating out our very own, unique waves of energy. Therefore, it is safe to say that this Universe is a gigantic, vibrating web of energy waves and we are here to be Master Wave Riders!

So, Magick happens by manipulating these waves utilizing the Universal Laws and the power of your intention and will. It is the practice of pure Magick in its most powerful form.

The modern day W.I.T.C.H is deeply connected and uses a combination of ancient traditions and proven quantum physics and science to manipulate and materialize (manifest) her desires.

It is where ancient wisdom meets modern day quantum invocation, or in other words; some serious Manifesting Magick.

This is true Magickal Mastery. Harnessing your own power and using the secrets of the Universe to manifest without the hustle, without the struggle and without the doubt.

Magic, miracles, and the practice of being limitless are the three secret ingredients that I hold dear to my heart, and I would love for you to embrace these elements in your life. Knowing on all levels that everything is truly possible.

Working with the Universal Laws is a precise practice. Each law entwining with another in alignment.

This is the key to creating Magick and Miracles in your life.

The Laws are consistently working for you, and it is up to you to attune your own energy and frequency with these Laws. Understanding the laws, the frequencies and your energy systems are important when looking at healing or manifesting in any area of your life: health, finances, relationships, romance – absolutely everything comes back to your energy system and your DNA, like a carefully woven spell; an intricate pattern of precision.

The powerful, Magickal Activation spells and invocations I create are the command that will manipulate and shift your energy to create the change in your life.

Modern spell work can heal any aspect in your life as it leads you to the root cause of the problem or block – unlocking and releasing it - just like magic; opening a pathway to reconnect your own Spiritual and Magickal gifts. I call this – Spellweaving. It will take you from strength to strength as you recover and reactivate more of your power and intuition.

The thing to remember here is that each of us is made from the spark of Magick that is the Universe, we contain stardust and cosmic energies that are yet to be fully understood on a scientific level.

You are far more than the eye can see. You are an eternal flame of energy that can never be distinguished. As a woman it is time to fully embrace all that you are truly capable of.

You are POWERFUL. You are MAGICKAL. You are a GODDESS. It is your BIRTHRIGHT.

Magick is a part of my daily life just as it was over 1000 years ago. Magick is an intrinsic part of who I am, it is not a separate thing I practice. I consider it a lifestyle and I live my life accordingly, not unlike someone who chooses a vegan lifestyle, a Christian lifestyle or a green lifestyle.

All Magick happens through will. The intention we have and our desire to achieve it. The greatest lie we have been taught is that we are not powerful. Especially as women, we have been indoctrinated into a submissive state of being, so we find manifesting far more difficult than our male counterparts who have been taught to be leaders, dominant and powerful (all perceived male traits).

With my private clients I see women from all walks of life, and all of them have had at some point some difficulty with manifesting. Some could rarely bring towards them what they wanted, others would be in a cycle of manic manifesting one month to zilch the next – from feast to famine, leaving them exhausted and burnt out, and others were great manifesters in one area of their lives but not in other areas.

All of these manifesting types are caused by the same underlying issue. The imbalance of their energy and frequency, and their beliefs.

If you are creating low frequency thoughts they will produce low frequency results and events in your life.

Remember the highest frequency is love and the moment you choose love over the doubt, fear, worries, you are choosing to connect to the frequency of the Divine – the frequency of creation and you lift your own frequency to the level of miracles.

CONNECTING

To begin, you must release the old paradigms and perceptions that have kept you trapped and unable to create and manifest at full power. What beliefs do you have as a woman? How do you experience life as a woman? What were the beliefs passed down to you as a child?

Depending on your starting point: where you are at in your own reconnection (awakening), there are many ways to shift through and release old limiting beliefs and energies.

Journaling, meditation and yoga are examples of ways to connect within, but I prefer the direct method I have created because it is faster, more powerful and effective.

As a starting point in my private practice, I take my clients through a massive release of persecution energy that exists at some level in every woman on this planet. Not only does this help you on your own personal level, but it feeds into the collective consciousness of all women and helps serve the planet and women at the highest level.

Partaking in this is truly powerful and will release you and your ancestors from persecution, repression, shame, and torture and will re-establish and activate your dormant DNA.

You will feel different. And if you feel energy already, you may even feel a release perhaps in the form of yawning, burping, emotions, or tingling energy running throughout your body.

Everyone experiences a release in different ways, so don't be disheartened if you don't appear to feel or experience anything – trust and know this is working on a level you cannot see, and as your intuition grows so too will your clairsentience (your feeling).

Connecting to your inner W.I.T.C.H is a process. In this book I will take you through the first steps in reconnection. Remember building your intuition and using your Magick is always a work in progress, and although I have formulated a way to fast track this for you, it will always depend on you feeling into what feels right for you.

WITCH tip:

This is also a part of you learning to tap into your intuition and discernment.

BEFORE YOUR START

It is important to always open a safe space to work within if you are performing any clearings or activations, and to close this space when you are finished.

Below are an opening and closing statement to use to connect into Source Energy and the power of the Universe, to powerfully shift your energy and then purify and cleanse your new energy field.

This will always ensure your upgrades and shifts last, and your space is kept free of unwanted energies or negative residue.

Use the opening statement before you use any Magick to ensure you have a sacred space in which to work. When you have finished clearing and activating always close down and cleanse your space using the closing statement.

Opening Sacred Space

I (your name) now allow myself to be a pure, clear conduit and connection to all that exists. I call upon the assistance of Divine Source Energy and the Divine power of the Golden Ratio including the 5 elements of the Pentagram – Earth, Air, Fire, Water and Spirit. I unlock the words of power – Arom Nahrea, Keli, Lekab, Sael, Vaho, Doni, Aumen, Mabeh, Aiau, Arom Nahrea and I seal my intentions with love and blessings.

Thank you, thank you, thank you.

Closing Sacred Space

I request cleansing and closure of all gateways of access to all other dimensions and realities.

I release all thought forms, beings or energies that are no longer of service to my highest good, across all planes of my existence, across all Universes, all lifetimes and all dimensions of time and space.

I give thanks to all those who assisted me, and I ask that all energies less than love now be transmuted for the highest good of all.

And so, it is.

FIRST LET ME EXPLAIN THE WORDS OF POWER

Before taking you through this clearing and activation, I would like to take the time to explain some of the words and the power that they hold.

Every incantation will begin with a request of connection with the Divine. Every incantation or command will end with a closing and sealing of the channel.

All Magick and miracles come through us in unity with the Divine Creator. We are the channel in which the power can move through. You need to be in alignment with your power, in your highest frequency to connect with your manifesting potential.

Every request is a request for Divine Blessings and Grace, so our intention needs to be pure for the Magick to work in its most powerful form and for the best and highest good of all.

Words have immense power when set with intention, and in this invocation, you call upon the Words of Power. The Words of Power you will be using are from the 72 Names (Angels) Of God and you will call upon this Angelic power and assistance.

Arom Nahrea is the mantra used to unlock the power of the Words. Each word (Angel) is numbered 1-72 in the Kabbalah. You will use the following 9. (I have placed their corresponding numbers next to them for reference purpose if you would like to further research these Angels).

18. Keli
31. Lekab
34. Lehah
45. Sael
49. Vaho
50. Doni
52. Aumem
55. Mabeh
67. Aiau

Please do not worry too much about how you pronounce the names as everyone pronounces them differently depending on voice, pitch, and ethnicity. The Angels always hear your requests when you open yourself up to asking for assistance and this is the most powerful way I know, to get instant access.

All my spells and invocations are extremely powerful and prolific and even more so when using the Words of Power.

My express intention for each of you using this guide book, is for you to increase your intuition, so every invocation and command is designed for you to receive maximum downloads that you can utilize to further your own Ascension, bringing you closer to your Divine birthright and your WITCH power.

So please, join with me in the following invocations and activations to connect you to your inner WITCH.

CLEANSE AND UPGRADE YOUR DNA BLOODLINES AND ANCESTRAL LINES AND ACTIVATE YOUR W.I.T.C.H DNA.

Make sure you are in a space where you will not be disturbed, set the scene. Feel free to light some candles, play soft, soothing music, burn essential oils, hold or place crystals around you, whatever feels right, allow yourself to be guided by your own intuition and what you connect with. The purpose of setting the scene is to assist you to drop into a space that you will relax enough to allow your higher self to take control. If you find it difficult to relax, invite your spirit to step forward and take charge of your body.

Now take some deep breaths before you start, just centring your energy, and as you exhale let go of any tension, stress or negative thoughts or emotions that are lingering.

Imagine, feel, or perceive a brilliant white light now streaming down through the top of your head (your crown chakra) and this luscious liquid light is now filling your entire body with pure white light.

Your body and soul are now beaming with unconditional love and abundance!

Open your sacred space.

I (your name) now allow myself to be a pure, clear conduit and connection to all that exists. I call upon the assistance of Divine Source Energy and the Divine power of the Golden Ratio including the 5 elements of the Pentagram – Earth, Air, Fire, Water and Spirit. I unlock the words of power – Arom Nahrea, Keli, Lekab, Sael, Vaho, Doni, Aumen, Mabeh, Aiau, Arom Nahrea and I seal my intentions with love and blessings.

Thank you, thank you, thank you.

Please read this out loud with intention:

"In the Name of The Divine Creator of All, in the name of our Sacred Earth, the keepers of imprints in my ancestral lineage, I (your name) request the powers of Divine Light, Divine Love and Divine Mercy to bless my entire genealogic tree, to the very heart of my roots with Divine forgiveness and grace.

May this blessing be bestowed upon my ancestors, releasing them from old wounds, patterns, and compulsive, negative behaviours back to the origin of conception to obtain zero-point energy on all time, space and dimensions.

Transmuting, purifying, and alchemizing all generational curses, contracts, all persecution energy stored in my DNA bloodlines and Ancestral lines, all shame, guilt, and torture, including all the negative aspects of these actions into Luminous Light and Unconditional Love.

I bear witness today as the representative of my lineage, and I acknowledge our deeds and our faults, in words and thoughts, actions and failures, negative attitudes and beliefs, and I release all the negativity from all the generations that came before me, into Mother Earth for transmutation as I now integrate, perfect and restore the generational lines to the original beauty that they were always meant to be and represent.

Using the words of power: Arom Nahrea - Keli, Lekab, Lehah, Sael, Vaho, Doni, Aumem, Mabeh, Aiau - Arom Nahrea.

I command:

- My full DNA Identity record activation.
- Activation of my organic DNA codings.
- Activation of my WITCH DNA including all my spiritual gifts and powers.
- Alignment of the cosmic sovereign law and Krystal spiral flows of unity intelligence
- Activation of my Human 12 Tree Grid – the tree of life.
- Opening of the Crystalline seals and activation of my dormant DNA.
- Raise in vibration into the new Bliss Blueprint.
- Full energy, clarity, and body alignment.
- Strengthening of neurological circuitry to hold more light.
- Opening of more channels for higher self-embodiment.

- Activation of my heart-mind connection.
- Activation of the Sophianic body.
- Activation of the sacred Merkabah source energy and star.
- Activation of the ascension vehicle.
- Full embodiment of the avatar Christ body and monad oversoul.
- Activation of unity consciousness.

I now command the full reconnection of my sound and light bodies, activation of the diamond grid and 144 harmonics for full restoration and unification of the male and female energies within my planetary body.

I now choose to live in alignment with the universal laws embodying my true Divine essence, to live in abundance, health, joy and oneness and sovereignty from this time forwards.

And so, it is.

Thank you, thank you, thank you Divine. Thank you for this blessing".

Take some deep breaths – as you breathe in feel your heart fill with unconditional love and as you breathe out feel all heaviness or tension release from your body.

Congratulate yourself, you have just released centuries of persecution and dissolved generations of negative conditioning being passed along your bloodlines. You have activated your inner W.I.T.C.H DNA and opened to your spiritual gifts and powers.

Over the next few days ensure you are drinking plenty of fresh, filtered water to help continue the detox and release from the Etheric, Astral, Mental and Causal Bodies.

Make sure to note down or journal any changes you notice in the coming days and weeks, these could be big or small changes. This helps to build your intuition as you begin to see and feel the changes and recognize how your body and energy system reacts and feels.

We are all unique so please take the time to chart how you are progressing.

> **WITCH tip:**
>
> Use the example journal in the magic toolbox section.

GETTING INTO A HIGHER FREQUENCY - ACTIVATING UNCONDITIONAL LOVE.

Now that you have cleansed generations of persecution from your DNA it is time to get into a higher frequency and practice holding yourself in this higher frequency.

The higher the frequency, the faster manifestations appear in your 3D reality.

I suppose the first thing is to explain what *high frequency* is.

The easiest way to explain high frequency is simply anytime you feel good.

Think about a time when you felt happy, full of love or joyous. What were you doing? What was happening?

Maybe you were out walking in nature, watching a comedy, the birth of a child, a win, or when you were chatting with your girlfriends. These feel good frequencies are high vibes.

On the other hand, lower frequencies make you feel low, or bad. Think about the times you have felt sad, angry, or sick.

Another extremely crucial point is to look at the people that you are surrounding yourself with. What is their frequency like? If you have a surplus of friends, family or colleagues around you who are more often in a low frequency - complaining, criticizing, degrading, or simply jumping from one disaster to another, it is high time to look at releasing some of those energies from your energy circle. Time to let some of them go, even if it is painful now, it will be far more painful for you if you don't! Not only does your frequency affect you, but the frequency of those that are around you the most. Remember everything is energy. Whenever you identify or feel a low frequency it is best to move away from it. Protecting your energy is self-love and is imperative to keeping you in your highest frequency and in your power.

Look at this chart that shows the frequencies on a scale – showing the lowest vibrations. Some of the emotions may surprise you at how low they vibrate. This chart is a simple check guide to see how high you are vibing.

This chart is the Map of Consciousness, developed by David R. Hawkins. The Map of Consciousness is based on a logarithmic scale that spans from 0-1000.

Name of Level	Energetic "Frequency"	Associated Emotional State	View of Life
Enlightenment	700-1000	Ineffable	Is
Peace	600	Bliss	Perfect
Joy	540	Serenity	Complete
Love	500	Reverence	Benign
Reason	400	Understanding	Meaningful
Acceptance	350	Forgiveness	Harmonious
Willingness	310	Optimism	Hopeful
Neutrality	250	Trust	Satisfactory
Courage	200	Affirmation	Feasible
Pride	175	Scorn	Demanding
Anger	150	Hate	Antagonistic
Desire	125	Craving	Disappointing
Fear	100	Anxiety	Frightening
Grief	75	Regret	Tragic
Apathy	50	Despair	Hopeless
Guilt	30	Blame	Evil
Shame	20	Humiliation	Miserable

Remember frequencies attract frequencies, like attracts like. This is the Law of Attraction.

So, the next step is to get into a high vibe easily without having to "fake" it.

The following invocation will help activate unconditional love (the frequency of 528hz) throughout your entire energy system – YOU!

This will keep you high on the vibing scale and will help elevate you every day.

Notice how the energy feels as it begins to flow through you and set the intention to be impervious to any frequency less than this love. Unconditional love is your birthright and is the great healer of all.

So please, join with me in the following invocation.

Before you begin, if you have not already, open your sacred space and ensure you are somewhere you will not be disturbed. As always, feel free to light some candles, play soft, soothing music, hold or place crystals around you, whatever feels right, allow yourself to be guided by your own intuition.

UNCONDITIONAL LOVE ACTIVATION

Closing your eyes, getting really relaxed and comfortable now, taking a deep breath in and as you breathe out just allow any tension to leave your body.

A channel of gold shimmering pure white light is now entering the top of your head through the crown chakra) and is streaming down into every cell of your body.

You are relaxed, safe, and calm.

Please read this out loud:

"Dear Divine Loving source,

Please let me release any frequency less than love now.

Allow me to let go of all negative thoughts, feelings and beliefs that are not in my highest good.

I request full removal of all blocks, programs and implants restricting my connection.

I now allow myself to release all conditions I placed upon myself and my worth.

I release myself from these conditions fully.

Please connect me into unconditional love and activate the frequency of 528hz.

Pure, unfettered, boundless and whole.

True love, forever and unchanging.

All four loves - affection, friendship, romance, and unconditional love.

Unconditional love is pure and selfless. Divine loving oneness."

Feel yourself relax, melt, let go and surrender into this state of oneness. Into pure unconditional love.

See this love now filling your heart.

Allow your heart chakra to open fully, breaking open to reveal your true self.

In all your pain, fear, doubts and worries, and in all your beauty, strength and truth, as the angels now come in to assist and take away the stresses, allowing only the nourishment of unconditional love to completely fill the heart space now and connect you deeply into your true essence.

Unconditional love now travels throughout each and every cell, bringing a tingling, bubbly, sparkling energy throughout your entire body.

You are content, fulfilled, nurtured, and feel incredible love coursing through your veins, pumping from your heart and spreading all around your body to the very tips of your fingers and toes.

Place your hands over your heart now and pull your awareness back into this space as your heart whispers messages of positivity, joy, and deep, deep love to you now.

You are loved.
You are adored.
You are cherished.
You are precious.
You are safe.
You are supported, always.
You are a Divine creation and you are beaming with love.

Please read the following out loud:

"I (your name) confirm my heart chakra is now cleared, cleansed and activated and is now vibrating to the 528hz frequency of pure unconditional love.

I choose to stay connected to this vibration, to live in my power consistently, from this moment forwards.

And so, it is.

Thank you, thank you, thank you Divine".

Thank you for taking this time to honour your divinity and to nurture and support yourself. Love, blessings, and miracles in abundance. Big high fives to you right now.

Feel into how this energy feels within your body. Pretty amazing – right!

Over the next 4 weeks I want you to practice moving away from any frequency that feels less than what you are feeling right now. Remember this feeling and keep it stored within your mind and body and set the intention to return to this feeling or higher every morning as you open your eyes.

Allow the love to flow through, put your hands on your heart and draw your awareness within.

Repeat these affirmations while you have your hands on your heart and your awareness is focused on this space within:

I am loved.
I am adored.
I am cherished.
I am precious.
I love the woman I am and the woman I am becoming.
I am a powerful W.I.T.C.H (Woman in total control of herself).

> **WITCH tip:**
>
> If you have some rose quartz crystals, I encourage you to either hold one in your left hand and/or place it over your heart as it will increase the power of this activation.

Step 3: UNDERSTANDING THE UNIVERSAL LAWS

The Law of Attraction gets all the glory, but did you know it's not the only universal law?

Most have heard of the Law of Attraction but what is shared about this Law is only a snippet of how all the Laws work in unison with one another.

The Universal Laws are the true magic of life and this is what the "wise women" were intrinsically aware of. The Universal Laws play one of the most important parts in manifestation.

The fundamental Laws work in alignment with one another, and you need to align yourself and your energy system to them. This is true alignment and flow.

This is enlightenment.

There are 105 documented universal spiritual laws. All creation is governed by law.

The principles that operate in the outer Universe, the ones scientists have been able to discover, are called natural laws.

But there are more subtle laws that are in play in the spiritual planes and the inner realm of consciousness. The true nature of matter is held within these Laws.

I will cover 25 of these Laws and have chosen the major influencers when connecting to your inner W.I.T.C.H.

Be mindful of Universal Law in relation to self and to others, and know that in love all life is given, in love all things move.

Please do not be overwhelmed by the information. Take your time to read through the Laws and you will see that each of them generally fits together with logic, and flow on from one another.

It is imperative to take the time to understand these Laws as they are the basis in which all life revolves around and will make manifesting in flow your usual mode of operation; it will become a way of life, rather than a "fake it till you make it" type of experience.

I have never believed in the "fake it" mentality (after trying it and failing miserably every time) that many manifestation experts talk about. I believe we must feel the emotion, feel the frequency, to embody it before we can truly manifest with ease, grace, and flow. And it really is simple when you connect to your inner power and knowing.

The laws of nature do not apply only to Earth. Our entire Universe follows the same laws; and these laws never change.

Your cup of tea left on the bench will always become cool. Gravity remains steady, never random and the speed of light is constant. The Earth rotates in 24 hours. The Universe is orderly. It is precise. Scientists are still searching for the answer to exactly why that is. The law of physics is a pattern that nature obeys without exception.

Scientists today take for granted the idea that the Universe operates according to laws.

James Trefil's principle of universality states that "The laws of nature we discover here and now in our laboratories are true everywhere in the Universe and have been in force for all time."

Learning to live in accordance with the Universal laws will bring you a happier and more fulfilled life.

You will let go of resistance and be in flow. You will have more certainty and less confusion.

You will feel supported as you use them to navigate your life. Remember the law of physics – all of nature follows this pattern without exception, so the more we resist the more the block (problem) persists.

Here is a look at the 25 universal laws and how to use them.

Please take time to read these, review them often until they become familiar to you. Knowing, understanding, and using these laws alongside your Magick is the most powerful way to manifest without exception. I have placed the laws in this specific order as I feel it is a more natural flow from one to another and will be easier to shift from one to another and see the way in which they work in unison with each other.

UNIVERSAL LAW NO.1

The Law of Divine Oneness

Separation is an illusion. The Law of Divine Oneness is the foundational law, according to which absolutely everything in our Universe is interconnected. Meaning - every choice, word, desire, and belief you have will also have an impact on the world, and on the people in your life. This impact can be immediate and obvious sometimes, and at other times, it may take a while to manifest, or you may never ever even discover that it has occurred.

Try to think of yourself as part of everything around you to live in accordance with this law.

We are all one, and awareness of this makes us more powerful as well as more empathetic.

UNIVERSAL LAW NO.2

Law of Vibration

Everything is energy! According to the Law of Vibration, every particle in the Universe is in constant movement and constantly carries energy.

This applies to every part of the Universe, like the planets and stars and it also applies to the chair you are sitting on.

In addition to this, everything has its own specific energy frequency. So high energy particles are naturally attuned to other high energy particles, and the same is so for low energy particles. (The Law of Attraction in play).

Energy can only transform, never die. It must go forward or back, but it can never stand still because that is stagnation. The only thing we have control over is the level of vibration. If you want to attract higher energy you need to raise your vibration.

UNIVERSAL LAW NO.3

Law of Correspondence

As above, so below! This law is directly related to the foundational Law of Divine Oneness. The key here is that patterns repeat throughout the Universe, and that prominent patterns can also be found repeating on a very small scale. As an example, think of the Fibonacci code; the spiral pattern that reappears in all of nature and all throughout the galaxy. This is the Divine proportion 1.618.

Become aware of the patterns in your own life and in your thinking and notice how they repeat elsewhere in the world. As you do this, consider the kinds of pattern changes you might be able to make, and how those will create change on a large scale.

UNIVERSAL LAW NO.4

Law of Forgiveness

We cannot be forgiven until we forgive others. If you continue to cling to negative thoughts of anger, judgement, hatred, and intolerance against others, you cannot be happy. This law works with the energy of allowing and seeing all as love, to be able to let go of the unnatural feeling of getting even. The old energy of an eye for an eye keeps your vibration very low. To forgive, to release old anger, allows grace to relinquish karma stored in the akasha.

UNIVERSAL LAW NO.5

Law of Attraction

Like attracts Like. So, to have the things you desire in life, you must work out how to vibrate on the same frequency as these things. The Law of Attraction works closely with what I like to call the Mother of all laws, the Law of Frequency Harmony.

The more general lesson here is that being positive, proactive and loving, attracts more of the same into your life. Remember those high vibes! Meanwhile, pessimism, fear, anger, hate, lethargy will lead you to generate more negative experiences in all aspects of life.

By working to live more positively even just today, you are already using the Law of Attraction to create a better existence for yourself.

UNIVERSAL LAW NO.6

Law of Inspired Action

Actions are simply energy in motion. Law of Attraction practitioners regularly say that they wish they had known about the Law of Inspired action at an earlier stage! These two laws are tightly bound together, and the Inspired Action law tells us that we must actively and intuitively pursue our goals.

Many people think that visualizing a goal and developing a positive attitude towards is sufficient for the Law of Attraction to work in their favour.

Inspired action is action that supports our desires and goals and that kind of action is always required for manifestation. You cannot just sit back and wait for the miracle! You need to take some action to get it moving. Remember the action you take needs to be inspired. Inspiration comes from our Divine Feminine so let her intuitively guide you into the action that feels inspirational to you.

UNIVERSAL LAW NO.7

Law of Perpetual Transmutation of Energy

Every single one of us has the power to change our reality through transmutation. The Law of Perpetual Transmutation of Energy states that everything around us is in constant flux. You cannot see all these changes because many of them exist at the cellular or atomic level, but they carry on regardless of whether we can see them or not. The reason that it is so important to be aware of this Law is that it helps you see how you can trigger positive change.

Specifically, keep in mind that high vibrations can trigger improvements in low vibrations. For example, if you are vibrating at a low frequency, exposing yourself to the high frequency of a happy, encouraging friend will naturally trigger energy transmutation in you.

Creating a higher vibration allows us to transmute the lower ones. It is all up to you to make the effort to change your own life.

UNIVERSAL LAW NO.8

Law of Cause and Effect

Every action we take has a reaction or consequence. One of the most straightforward laws of the Universe, the Law of Cause and Effect tells us that all actions have a corresponding reaction. You will already know this, of course, when it comes to the physical aspects of the world. However, perhaps you have not considered how this law might be applied to the spiritual aspects of our Universe.

Your spiritual life can impact the world around you, causing positive or negative reactions. Similarly, your physical environment can impact on your spirituality, whether for good or for ill. Ask yourself what types of relationships you see between the spiritual and the physical, and how you might want to change them.

Your thoughts, behaviours, and actions create specific effects that manifest and create your life as you know it. If you are not happy with the result you have created, then you must change the that created it in the first place.

Change your actions, and you change your life... Transform your thoughts, and you will create a brand-new destiny.

UNIVERSAL LAW NO.9

Law of Compensation

We reap what we sow. According to the Law of Compensation, you will receive what you put out. This is like the Law of Attraction, but with a focus on the idea that compensation can come in many forms. For example, if you win a large amount of money then you might think you are getting a reward. However, depending on how you have lived, your vast amount of wealth could lead to a worse life rather than a better one. Money is an amplifier so is not always a windfall. It could be a blessing or a very big lesson. Essentially, you reap what you sow, and you get back what you put out.

So basically, you cannot take negative action and not expect to feel some kick-back!

It is always wise to consider the true consequences of your actions. This law reminds you to be careful about how you treat others, and indeed the planet.

UNIVERSAL LAW NO.10

Law of Relativity

It is all in the perception. The Law of Relativity is all about the neutrality of things when seen in isolation. So, no person, experience, emotion, or action is evaluated as good or bad until you look at it in comparison with something else. For example, you may think you are poor, but perhaps that is because you have three wealthy relatives.

By keeping this law in mind, you remain conscious of the fact that there are always multiple perspectives on anything that happens to you. Trying to slip into these alternate perspectives can make you more grateful and can also show you where you can make improvements in life. Perception is everything. Stop comparing.

UNIVERSAL LAW NO.11

Law of Polarity

Opposites are just two extremes of the same thing. Night and day, above and below, dark and light, masculine and feminine, yin and yang. The Law of Polarity tell us that absolutely everything has an opposite and that it is the very existence of these opposites that allow us to understand our life.

They may differ by degrees, but they occupy the same spectrum. Finding a balance between the two ends is usually the best way to create a happy existence.

When you go through something difficult, it will be this thing that helps you truly appreciate the good developments to come.

Find the lesson and the blessing and be grateful.

UNIVERSAL LAW NO.12

Law of Rhythm

Life will always ebb and flow. Sometimes called the Law of Perpetual Motion, the Law of Rhythm is focused on movement. Referring to the fact that all things come in cycles.

You can see this in nature, e.g., in the seasons, and in the body's aging process. However, it equally applies to a person's life stages, and reflecting on this helps you to gain perspective.

It moves with the years, the seasons, the stages of development, El Nino. It is unrealistic to expect things to only move on fast-forward. Surrender and settle in, move with the currents, not against them for maximum flow and ease.

UNIVERSAL LAW NO.13

Law of Gender

Everything has both masculine and feminine energy, yin and yang. The attraction between the two is how creation happens. We all contain a certain amount of both energy and must find a way to achieve a balance between our Divine Masculine and Divine Feminine if we are to live authentically and happily.

Think about the role each type of energy appears to play in your life, and whether there is an excess or a deficit of either.

UNIVERSAL LAW NO.14

Law of Charity

The more you give away, the more you receive. When you are generous, you will receive generosity back. Giving help (financial or otherwise) will never deplete you; that energy will come back to you even stronger. You will always be rewarded for your acts of charity. Live in generosity consciousness.

UNIVERSAL LAW NO.15

Law of Reflection

We see the traits in others that exist in ourselves. The Law of Reflection states that everything you see is only a mirror reflection of that which is within you.

This is one of the hardest laws to understand and accept because it forces us to take responsibility for our own energy. Most people like to think that it is outside people or circumstances that are causing them to be happy or angry.

Since everything is vibration it is you who is attracting these external situations to you.

Hence, that individual who irritates you has come into your life because that is an active vibration within you. That irritable person is mirroring that which exists within you. When working with the Law of Reflection, it is important to understand that sometimes the mirror may not be a direct reflection of what is within you. It may reflect your opposite. If you are overly kind, through that kindness, you tend to attract people and situations that will take advantage of that kindness. Look at where your kindness is being motivated by guilt or by a need to have people like you. Being kind is not always an honourable trait as we are forgetting to value and appreciate ourselves.

UNIVERSAL LAW NO.16

Law of Fellowship

Combining our efforts with those around us allows us to generate a bigger and better outcome. When two people of similar vibrations unite for a purpose, their energy is more than doubled towards that goal. Look for ways you can harness and amplify this energy. Finding more like-minded friends is a wonderful first step. Collaboration is powerful!

UNIVERSAL LAW NO.17

Law of Unconditional Love

Expressing unconditional love results in a harmonious life. But to be clear, unconditional love is a lot bigger than romantic love! It is about accepting the people in your life exactly the way they are without judgment or expectation. It does not involve changing people or using them to your benefit! It is all about pure acceptance.

Love without condition and watch your life transform as you attract more of the same to yourself.

UNIVERSAL LAW NO.18

Law of Evolution

There is no real death. Death is just another up level for the soul. We are continually evolving at the soul level and evolution is infinite. On the surface it might not appear that you are making progress at times, but your soul is always growing and expanding.

Every experience – even mistakes and failures – are allowing your soul to expand.

UNIVERSAL LAW NO.19

Law of Initiation

Expect an initiation period, a time of learning before things come together. Everyone experiences challenges in life, even when you are on the right path!

You are challenged for a reason so use these challenges as an opportunity to learn and grow. They have been brought to you to make you, or your mission, even stronger.

UNIVERSAL LAW NO.20

Law of Harmony

Harmony is the opposite of chaos; it is the ultimate balance in life and the purpose of Karma.

Throwing a rock in a pond will create ripples for a while (disharmony) until everything settles back into its natural harmonious state. Doing disharmonious acts does the same thing, only instead of spreading harmonious energy out you are spreading disharmony.

Harmony works closely with the Law of Cause and Effect and the Law of Attraction. So, if you find yourself jumping on the drama train, it may be wise to get off at the next stop!

UNIVERSAL LAW NO.21

Law of Resistance

What you resist persists. You cannot stick your head in the sand and ignore your life!

Failing to acknowledge a situation means you are not really stepping up and dealing with it.

And attempting to avoid it means it is not going to go away. Resistance is fear and you must learn to conquer your fear if you want to resolve your issues.

UNIVERSAL LAW NO.22

Law of Manifestation

Thoughts and feelings plus inspired action = manifestation. Everything that we have created began as a thought. If you want to change your life, the change begins inside your own head and energy field. You must dream of it before it can ever happen.

The limits you put on yourself are the only things holding you back.

UNIVERSAL LAW NO.23

Law of Prosperity

The Law of Prosperity states that when one prospers, all prosper. Your level of prosperity will be in direct proportion to your responses about another person's prosperity. Most people do not understand that if you are secretly taking private pleasure in another person's misfortune or begrudging another person's prosperity, you are affecting your own possibilities of generating prosperity. Everything works on vibration. The feelings of jealousy and resentment you harbor about another's well-being will keep you locked into a lower vibrational frequency of lack. Smile upon someone else's success and good fortune, and you are smiling upon your own.

UNIVERSAL LAW NO.24

Law of Belief

The thoughts you hold in your mind influence your world. Your words, feelings and behaviour also affect the world around you and y beliefs (conscious or not).

Believing subconsciously that rich people are morally bankrupt or that there are no good single men left in the world will result in those things becoming your reality.

Become mindful of your internal beliefs. Look at where you hold strong negative beliefs, it is time to let them go.

UNIVERSAL LAW NO.25

Law of Divine Order

Everything is exactly as it should be! There are no accidents in life. There is no coincidence.

Every seemingly negative event leads us to a new path. All your experiences were meant to happen.

Accept them for what they are and for letting them shape your journey.

Please keep revisiting and practising these Laws until you build an understanding of each. They all work in unison with one another and all of them are affected by your frequency. It is super important to work on and practice keeping your frequency high, because overall these Laws all culminate in the "Law of Frequency Harmony".

The attunement of your frequency and vibration, shifting you into higher consciousness.

This is what you are here to master. Your own frequency and attune that frequency to the frequency of the Universe. The God Frequency. The Frequency of Enlightenment.

You too will learn how to attune your frequency and use it like a Magick wand as you unlock your inner W.I.T.C.H.

CHOOSE YOU

YOU ARE BEING ASKED TO CHOOSE TO
FEEL WORTHY OF BEING
DIVINELY LOVED.

KNOW THAT THE DIVINE UNCONDITIONALLY
LOVES YOU AND IS ASKING YOU NOW TO FEEL
THIS LOVE FOR YOURSELF.

OPEN YOUR HEART AND YOUR HANDS READY
TO RECEIVE THE LOVE YOU
ARE SO WORTHY OF.

AFFIRMATION:

I CHOOSE TO FEEL WORTHY
OF BEING LOVED.

CHAPTER 4

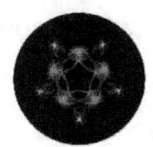

Start with LOVE for love is the beginning and the end.

Start at the beginning. Magick is far more than the casting of a spell or incantation. True Magick happens when we are loved up. Love is Power and Power is Love. There is no greater manifestor than this.

SELF LOVE

Self-love is far more than self-care. It is the complete and total acceptance of oneself in every form, both light and dark. It is letting go of self-judgement and negative self-talk and instead having complete forgiveness and compassion for yourself, your actions, and your experiences.

Embodying the frequency of love helps you to have compassion for all, including self. Self-Love is the beginning and it is the end. The infinite loop of life. Connecting into unshakeable self-love is important because it empowers you. It brings you closer to your infinite power centre. The heart-mind connection. This exists in all of nature.

Love is the frequency that is the glue of the Universe. It holds

everything together.

You have the power of miracles within you. You are the infinite creator in your life. You are in control whether you realize it or not. You are an angel as solidly as you are human. You came from pure love and will always remain pure love. The beginning and the end. Self-love is not arrogant, nor is it egotistical. It is the ultimate expression of all that is.

Loving self; equates to loving the Universe.

Self-love is also the key to unlock your innate power and Magick. To truly step into your W.I.T.C.H – Woman in total control of herself, you need to completely accept and love the human/spiritual/cosmic being you are. In all your light and your darkness. Full acceptance of the beautiful Goddess you are.

Remember those Universal Laws, in particular; the Law of Attraction - we attract that in which we vibrate.

In this chapter, we are going to look at how to begin to align your energy: your frequency. Because you create your life with the frequencies that you choose to attune to. The thing to remember here is that you may create your life any way that you choose. You are a free will being and are fully supported by the Universe in your choices, whether they are positive or negative. The Universe is always reflecting to you.

You may have the false belief that life happens to you; this is just an illusion. Life happens for you.

The only thing you can control in your life is you. You have no control over anything that is outside of you. Once you come to terms with this profound fact, you will find it far easier to allow the negative to release from your experiences, because you will understand that every experience you have in this life, you have created. You are the master. Embrace it. Every choice that you make is creating your life moment to moment. Your thoughts, your feelings, the words that you speak. Each of them carries a frequency that will either empower or disempower you.

> *"You always had the power my dear, you just had to learn it for yourself."* ~ Glinda

Considering that you are a being of free will, you have choice; choose wisely. Start by tapping into your own intuition, your own inner guidance. If you are new to connecting to your intuition, please do not be fooled by your emotions. Emotions are amazing guides for sure, but your emotions can be false representations of what is really going on, especially the lower controlling emotions like anger and fear. Anger and fear will guide you poorly in your day to day existence. Their real purpose is simply to lead you out of any physical type of danger, they are emotions that command a response from us immediately for your own safety. They are attached to the flight or fight response in your nervous system. They were never intended to consume your every waking moment and dictate decisions that you make in your life. When you are feeling these lower emotions of anger, fear, or shame, you make poor decisions in your life, and then these poor decisions manifest the experience you are having. Therefore, having an eject button on these emotions is crucial to your overall health and wellbeing.

You really must question everything. Discernment is key.

Use a system for yourself that will empower you and raise you above the false matrix of your current thoughts.

I teach muscle testing as a tool to each of my private clients as it is invaluable for tapping into your innate body wisdom and intelligence. And building trust in your intuition!

Muscle testing is a biofeedback mechanism. It works with the body's electrical/muscular relationship, which is a natural part of the human system, reading the body's balance through the balance of the electrical system at any given moment.

It assists you in accessing the subconscious mind by using the subconscious muscle responses as feedback. Through muscle testing questions, you can get answers from your subconscious mind. It can help you build your intuition and connect deeper into some of your unconscious thoughts and patterns. It is a great empowerment tool and can help you decipher if those energies or emotions you are feeling are yours or if indeed you may have taken them onboard from another, or even the collective consciousness. Most of our physical, emotional, and mental processing happens outside of our awareness, so this is a great way to dive deep and see what is happening at an unconscious level.

What you can use it for:

Primarily you are testing for what is in your body/mind/spirit's highest good at this moment in time. Here is a list of things I self-muscle test for in my own life.

Purchasing:

Is purchasing this item best for me at this time?
Menu items: Which dish on the menu is the best option for me?
Supermarket: Which brand of yoghurt is best for me? A, B, or C.

Choices:

Is it in my best interest to attend this women's circle or not?
What colour dress will I wear today to feel my best?
Is it in my best and highest good to purchase this or not?

Feelings/Emotions:

Is this emotion mine?
Is the emotion someone else's?
Am I ready to let go of this emotion?

And so on. There is no limit to what you can ask, and it will assist you to tap into your subconscious and your intuition as you build confidence in your own instinct and gut feelings.

HOW TO SELF- MUSCLE TEST

Bring your awareness into your hands. Form two intertwined circles with thumb and index fingers.

Start with your writing hand (or dominant hand) and place your thumb to your index finger. Then loop your other hand's thumb and index finger through the first "circuit". This creates the electrical circuit you will test the response with.

Firstly, you will begin by asking, "What is a YES answer for me"? Quickly pull your dominant hand away from the nondominant hand. Notice whether the fingers stay locked or unlock after you have asked the question.

Do this again by asking, "What is a NO answer for me"? Again, quickly pull your dominant hand away from the nondominant hand, noticing whether the fingers stay locked or unlock after you have asked the question. Be sure that the amount of pressure holding the circuit fingers together is equal to the amount of your testing fingers pressing against them. Use an equal and continuous pressure.

While learning, start by using practice questions. For example:

My name is (insert your name)
My name is (insert someone else's name)

I live in (insert your suburb or country)
I live in (insert a different suburb or country)

So, whilst holding your fingers "in circuit" ask the question … muscle test.

Please note - this is not a competition of strength! Just keep a light connection. You want to be relaxed and in flow when you ask the question.

WITCH

Example Diagram

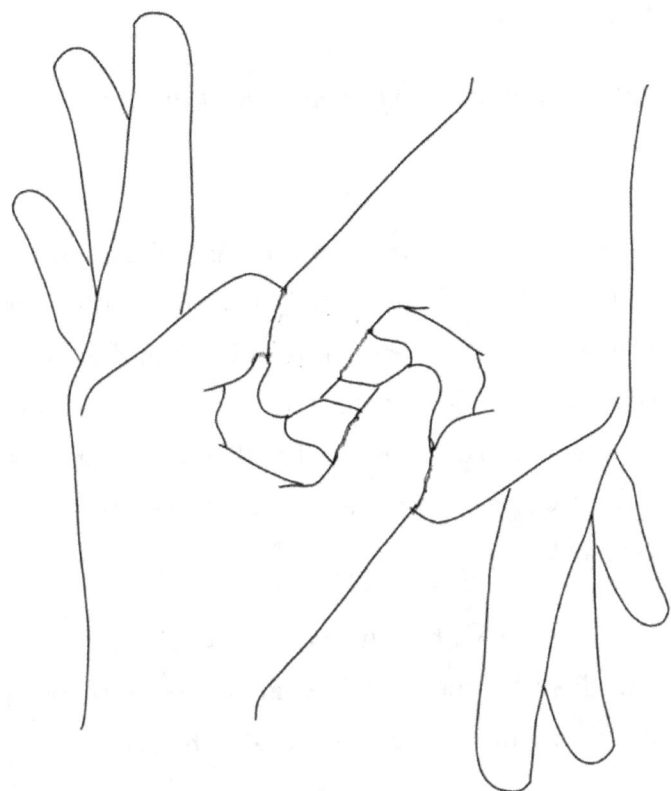

Once you have mastered this and feel confident in your Yes/No responses move on to questioning anything and everything.

Practice will build your confidence and your intuition will grow as you connect deeper with your subconscious. And as you connect deeper with your intuition you are simultaneously connecting deeper within your heart, your worth and value. This is the first step in actualizing self-love and acceptance. Keep up your practice with muscle testing as this will be helpful to you in chapter 6: Declutter your mind. Clearing limiting beliefs and self-sabotage.

So how do I attune my own frequency to that of 528hz – unconditional love?

Two things that are similar, or have the same frequency will form a connection, and resonate with each other in harmony. Like attracts like so similar frequencies will attract each other, and then they will harmonize together. In other words, light waves that vibrate to the same frequency will be drawn together. Therefore, you will draw things to in your life which reflect the frequencies that are in your very being, within your DNA, like attracts like.

You are creating your life with your frequency choices, and you are doing it in your life in this very moment. You are either consciously choosing frequencies, or you are unconsciously choosing frequencies. It is all up to you.

Everything you consume on any level has a direct effect on your frequency.

Take food as an example. Food that is closer to nature, that comes directly from the Earth and is unprocessed, holds a higher frequency, and has a higher life force energy. Those foods that are filled with this lifeforce energy, feed and revitalize the body. They nourish the soul, improve your mental state and regulate your hormones that directly control your emotions.

On the other hand, processed foods and junk food have a very low frequency and do not help your body at all, they fill it full of toxins, chemicals and damaging junk that attacks the cells. It gets collected in the organs and creates sickness or dis-ease within the body. The food you choose to put into your body will be reflected to you in your life through your health, your looks, your energy, and your weight. Food is a frequency too!

The next step you need to take, is to nourish your body energetically!

The following invocation will assist in attuning your frequency so you can truly feel Divine love within your body, filling you up and keeping you full. Filling your Divine Temple so that you can attune your frequency, at will, to this beautiful 528 hertz of unconditional love and continuously feel that very same love for yourself. This will assist you to keep choosing love, to keep going back to the source of this love, and filling your temple with this love, so that you can continuously make better choices, which will create a more joyful life for you, right now.

Feeling good, feeling loved, and appreciating yourself will allow you to move into your power far easier, without struggle as you continue to develop your inner W.I.T.C.H. So please, join with me in this following immersion.

Before you begin, if you have not already, open your sacred space and ensure you are somewhere you will not be disturbed. As always, free to light some candles, play soft, soothing music, hold or place crystals around you, whatever feels right, allow yourself to be guided by your own intuition.

The purpose of setting the scene is to assist you to drop into a space that you will relax enough to allow your higher self to take control. If you find it difficult to relax, invite your spirit to step forward and take charge of your body.

IMMERSION - FILLING MY TEMPLE WITH LOVE.

Focus on your breathing. In and out. Breathing in unconditional love and as you breathe out simply releasing all tension, fear, stress or worry. Deeply breathing allow yourself to relax completely.

Repeat aloud:

"Dearest Divine Loving Source of All that is, please now release all emotions that are not love with ease and grace. "

Place your hands over your heart space and bring your awareness into this space now.

See the light turn on in your heart and as it does the light becomes brighter and brighter as it expands further and further outwards from your heart space.

In this light you feel safe and you can now see that you are surrounded by angels, guides, enlightened beings, guardians, and your ascended masters, and they are all sending you their love, guidance, protection, and support.

They are here to heal you and fill you completely with Divine Love and Oneness.

This light expands and you realize that this light is your consciousness. This is where you can connect anytime.

It is a place where you are safe, a place where you feel peace, and a place where you feel love.

The light of your consciousness continues to expand past the heart and forms a huge bubble of light all around you.

Expanding your consciousness allows all of your problems and worries to simply fall away – to fall off the left side of your body and the right side of your body.

They simply vanish as you expand your perspective and fill with more love and light.

Enjoy floating in this light and expanding your consciousness and your awareness.

As you float in this light, this calmness, you feel the freedom and the peace of being connected to the Universe and to all of Mother Earth.

In the brilliant glow of the light, you can see all the people who have ever supported you, now walking towards you. They are all right there now in your presence, in your consciousness.

You look at their faces and you can feel their love healing you, you can feel it filling your heart and expanding it with pure joy and unconditional love.

Experience the power of what love can do and the power of healing that it has.

As you feel into this love, I want you to now think about all the love that you have given to those you love. And now send this enormous wave of love to your own heart and fill your heart with this incredible love so you can feel the very same love for yourself.

This is who you really are, this is who you are here to be, and this is what you are meant to experience.

Pure, unconditional love.

Now choose to be this love, to feel this love and to embrace this love. For you are so loved.
You are love.
You are cherished.
You are adored.
And you are precious.
You are fully supported by the Universe in Divine Love and Oneness.

Repeat aloud:

"Thank you, thank you, thank you, Divine.

And so, it is".

I encourage you to be brave, be confident and take a leap of faith in yourself. Follow your heart for she knows the way. Dream often, dream big and chase those dreams with passion.

"I see you. I hear you. I feel you. I love you".

CHOOSE YOU

YOU ARE BEING ASKED TO CHOOSE TO DO WHAT YOU LOVE.

LET GO OF THE EXPECTATIONS AND ALLOW YOURSELF TO FOLLOW YOUR PASSIONS.

DOING WHAT YOU LOVE CREATES MORE HAPPINESS AND JOY.

AFFIRMATION:

I CHOOSE TO DO WHAT I LOVE.

CHAPTER 5

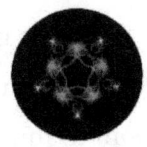

What exactly do I want?

Sometimes what you want and what is best for you may be two different things.

Therefore, the process of clearing out anything that stands in the way of you achieving your desired outcome needs to be undertaken. To begin I always encourage my clients to journal. To envision what they truly desire for their life, to get clear on their intentions and to get clear on who they truly are.

What really gets you excited and passionate enough to manifest it?

This can be a cathartic process. So much so, often your desire changes as you realize that you can be and have anything, that you truly are limitless, and the possibilities are endless. This brings with it a wave of excitement that will forever change your way of thinking.

GET MORE CLARITY ON WHAT YOU WANT IN YOUR LIFE.

I love setting home-play exercises for my private clients to get them clearer on what they really want and desire on a subconscious level, and I am going to share that with you now.

Please note - You can do these exercises more than once to dive deeper into your desires or if you are feeling unfulfilled by a previous desire or achievement. There is always room to improve, uplevel and call in more. You as we all are, are constantly evolving.

This is far more than a journaling exercise and involves rituals, releases and reprogramming to get you clearer on your desires. This is super powerful in helping you achieve a more positive mindset and assisting you to reprogram your neural pathways to create new experiences. When used in conjunction with the powerful invocations in this book, you will be well on your way to manifesting your heart's desires.

CREATE YOUR OWN LIFE STORY

The first thing to do is to write down all those things that no longer serve you. What are the things that are showing up in your life that you would like to change?

Make a list of all the beliefs and programs, "the rules", that you feel you should be doing.

Now with this list of "rules" you think you should be doing; I want you to look at each one and write down how each "rule" or belief makes you feel. Spend time feeling into the emotions and note down anything that comes up for you. Once you have your list and how the "rules" you feel, it is now time to surrender it all. This is the fun part!

All these old beliefs, programs, and rules you have been following in your life are no longer a part of who you are. You can consciously choose differently for yourself now. They are simply a rule book that you have been conditioned to believe. They are not truth. They never were.

So, it is time to let them go. You will do this by releasing them.

With your list in hand now repeat aloud:

"I now choose to release these old negative patterns, beliefs and rules (you can state your rules here). I instantly clear and transmute them with the power of unconditional love and forgiveness. I choose to make my own rules from this moment on and live in my full creative power.

And so, it is".

You can also choose to make this more power and perform this as a ritual. Under the moonlight with the stars as you witness, read the above release, and once you have finished, simply burn your list and surrender the energy to the all loving and supportive Universe and the blessings of the Divine Creator.

The choice is yours, either way it is a powerful way to let go and surrender into your beingness.

SO, I HAVE SURRENDERED. NOW WHAT?

The next part to this exercise is to create your circle of love. This is a drawing exercise, so it is completely up to your imagination; let your creative juices flow. Feel free to use colours and pens that represent your personality or what you want to feel.

On a piece of paper or in your journal, draw a big circle, making sure it fills the entire page. In the middle of the circle write the word LOVES. Make it as decorative or as bold as you like. Then fill the entire circle with everything that you love and enjoy and want to have and bring into your life. Keep going until you run out of space.

Then choose 5 things out of the circle and highlight them or put a circle around them. Choose the most important things that you would most like, so you can focus on these things first. You can repeat this exercise as often as you like and the more you do it, the less it represents the things you desire, and the more it begins to look like a mirror image of your actual life.

Great, so you have your desires down.

Now it is time to set some new beliefs and boundaries. You are going to be creating your own life story using your own rules. You get to choose. Your life, your way. By making new guidelines for yourself you are setting a powerful intention for your life. Choosing and creating the experiences you want to have.

Centring your focus on the way you want to feel you are opening new possibilities for yourself that you once thought you should not do or could not have. This is the power of creation. Intention is powerful and when we think and feel with intention, we become powerful manifestors of abundance. This abundance is our birthright- something that has been hidden from us for lifetimes.

Now you know what you love you are closer to knowing what you want in your life. The next part to this exercise is to set new "rules" for your life.

Make a list of all the beliefs and programs, "the rules", that you want to have in your life. What rules will serve you in experiencing life the way you want to? And what new beliefs and boundaries can you choose that will get you closer to feeling and experiencing your "loves'.

New rules, New YOU.

Time to put the new rules into practice. Each day practice these new rules. A great and powerful way to set these new rules in motion for you is to anchor lock these new rules, beliefs, and guidelines into your subconscious.

To do this, begin by getting relaxed, take some deep breaths, and centre yourself into your heart space. Have your list with you and light a candle. Focus on your list and read them aloud.

Then simply state out loud:

"I now anchor lock and seal these new programs, beliefs and rules throughout my hologram, anchor lock and seal through my subconscious, my DNA and the time matrix.

And so, it is".

Blow out the candle and place your list under your pillow or in your bedside drawers and read every night for the next 13 days. Keep practicing your new "rules", and you will find that within the next few weeks they will become your "normal" way of being. You will feel strengthened and free to just be you.

> **WITCH tip:**
>
> You could also put a crystal with your list either in your drawer or under your pillow. Choose either Citrine or Labradorite for your intentions.

GETTING CLEAR BY CONNECTING WITH YOUR SPIRIT GUIDES

Another way to get clear is to ask for the guidance from your spiritual team. First you will need to connect to them. Connecting to your spirit guides is about learning to trust that voice of love.

The reason your guides and your spiritual evolution team are here is to constantly bridge your thoughts from fear back to faith, for healing the mental, emotional and physical, for forgiveness, love and light and to help your soul evolve into your highest potential. They present you with creative solutions and beautiful opportunities bringing your attention to the possibilities and the magic that exists in your day to day life. They are your support system to get you moving and to assist you to fulfil your soul's mission.

My spiritual evolution team: who are they?

1. Spirit Guides

Spirit Guides were once human but have ascended to a higher level of consciousness to become angelic guides. They are assigned to you because they have a deep understanding of the soul lessons that you need to learn in this lifetime. They can also be a soulmate, an animal, or a loved one who has crossed over. They offer you guidance, support, and clarity to the situations in your life. They will never tell you what to do, but they will always guide you to the right answer.

2. Guardian Angels

Unlike Spirit Guides, Guardian Angels have never been human before and have only ever existed in Divine form. They are high energy beings who are here to protect and watch out for your soul on its earthly journey. They can be called upon when you need protection, or when you are feeling fearful or scared about a situation.

They can also offer comfort, guidance, and reassurance. Most of us have more than one Guardian Angel and can connect with them by simply inviting them in and staying opening and trusting to the signs that are received.

3. Archangels

Archangels are the master Angels and oversee all souls on Earth and even other Angels and Spirit Guides. They are of an extremely high vibration and can be evoked to help through any problem or issue, or when you need protection. No problem is too small for an Archangel! While Guardian and Spirit guides can sometimes be unique to the individual, everyone has access to the same Archangels.

Here is a list of the 15 Archangels and their areas of expertise.

1. Archangel Michael: a powerful archangel of protection, helps you to release fear, worry, clear negative energies, and find lost belongings.

2. Archangel Gabriel: the archangel of communication, new beginnings, and strength. Can help you to find your higher calling.

3. Archangel Metatron: is the Divine record keeper and a powerful spiritual teacher. Can help you to release and let go of the past and can help you tap into your Divine connection.

4. Archangel Raphael: the main archangel that oversees healing of all living creatures. Inviting him in can also help activate your own self-healing process.

5. Archangel Haniel: the archangel of energy, vitality, and passion. She can release lower vibrations and evoke healing and love.

6. Archangel Ariel: a powerful archangel that is can be called upon to evoke personal power and strength.

7. Archangel Muriel: the archangel of peace and harmony, she oversees emotions, unconditional love, and compassion. She can also help protect those with intuitive or empathic abilities.

8. Archangel Chamuel: the archangel of protection, peace, and compassion.

9. Archangel Zadkiel: the archangel of cleansing, forgiveness, and freedom. Can be called upon to help you raise your vibration and bring about forgiveness to a situation.

10. Archangel Azrael: assists souls in making the transition from physical life to the afterlife.

11. Archangel Uriel: the light of God, she is an illumination of light for all human souls. She represents openness and willingness to receive love and allows you to deepen your spiritual connection.

12. Archangel Jeremiel: the 'Mercy of God'. He assists with reviewing past events and obtaining clarity on the lessons and messages to be learnt to bring about emotional healing. He helps a person to view themselves and others with the intention of mercy and compassion and to apply forgiveness to bring more peace into the world. He also assists with access to the Akashic records to view and understand lessons of past lifetimes.

13. Archangel Jophiel: the 'Beauty of God'. Jophiel helps us to think more beautiful and kind thoughts. This assists with the creation and attraction of more kindness and beauty into our lives.

14. Archangel Raguel the 'Friend of God'. His main purpose is to oversee all the other archangels and angels, to ensure that they are all working together in a harmonious and organised manner. He is called upon when there is conflict, chaos, and disorganisation.

15. Archangel Raziel: the 'Secrets of God'. He is the 'Keeper of Secrets' and the 'Angel of Mysteries'. He works closely with God and knows the secrets of the Universe and how it operates. Archangel Raziel can help you understand esoteric material and increase your ability to see, hear, know, and feel Divine guidance.

Want to evoke the assistance of an Archangel?

The following invocation will connect you to the Archangel you would like guidance and assistance from. Use it to call upon the angels for support and to feel protection when you may be feeling vulnerable.

Say aloud:

"I request the assistance of Archangel (insert your angel's name) to help me with all I require at this time, and to shower me with their healing grace and powers, with blessings and love, magic and miracles. And that Archangel (insert your angel's name) will guide, protect and bring awareness to all the things that I require for my soul's advancement so I am blessed with experiences that are in my best and highest good. Please wrap your wings around me and offer me a safe place to fall and assist me in connecting with my infinite wisdom.

In gratitude I thank you Archangel (insert your angel's name) for accepting my request.

Thank you, thank you, thank you for bestowing your grace upon me.

And so, it is".

4. The Ascended Masters

Ascended Masters are those who were once human, like all of us, but paid off their karmic debt and mastered ascension. They no longer have a physical body, but unlike other spiritual beings like Spirit Guides or Angels, they once had one and can relate to the frustration of the karmic cycle. That means that each of us is essentially an Ascended master's in training.

Ascended Masters have a huge knowledge base that we can consult with. They have lived through the physical limitations of the reincarnation cycle and they have experienced the great power of higher dimensions. They work with each of us to guide us through the initiations of ascension.

Everyone has a Spirit Team which is always available at any time, no matter the circumstances or the level of enlightenment. It may seem simple but connecting with your Spirit Team is really about welcoming them into your life, keeping an open mind and trusting so you can remain open to their messages.

STEPS TO CONNECT TO YOUR SPIRIT GUIDES

Step 1: Start Asking!

The first step to connecting with your spirit guides is to get into the habit of asking. We often forget that we have guidance within us and around us. It is important that you start getting into the habit of asking your guides for help. The more you ask, the more you receive! Think about all the things that you need help with and start asking.

MAKE A LIST OF WHAT YOU NEED YOUR SPIRIT GUIDES' HELP WITH

Make a list of the 5 things you need help with right now.

Once you have made this list, offer up everything you need help with and invite in all your guides, enlightened beings of love and above and your spiritual evolution team for assistance and to provide solutions. Always thank your team of guides. Having an attitude of gratitude is the best way to receive more and show your appreciation.

You can use the following invitation to enlist the assistance and reconnect with your Spiritual Evolution Team.

Say aloud:

"I now invite my full spiritual evolution team including all guides, angels and ascended masters to connect with, offer assistance, guidance and healing to me as I may require. I give my full permission for my team to work closely with me to guide me back into alignment with the love of the Universe, to protect me and bring awareness to all the things that I need for my soul's advancement. I am hereby opening the channels of communication with my spiritual evolution team and with a grateful heart I acknowledge this connection and declare it so".

Call on your team anytime. You do not need to have a problem to talk to them. They are there to hear you out, offer assistance, comfort and support.

Step 2: Listen!

Listen. The way to do this is through meditation and/or breathing techniques.

When you meditate, or focus on your breathing, you quieten your mind so that you can hear the wisdom of the guidance that is within you and around you.

Step 3: Journal or write!

After meditating and listening, the next step is to explore and allow the free flow of writing or journaling around your problem. Many times, your team will work through you inspiring solutions through your written expression. You may even find your guides speak to you while you are writing inspiring great words of wisdom and guidance.

Step 4: Pay attention to the guidance you receive!

It is all great to ask for guidance, but the next step is to pay attention, witness the guidance and act upon it. There is no use in asking for a solution and then not following through. Paying attention to the guidance will also bring a feeling of support and nurturing and a beautiful feeling of unconditional love. Allow yourself the gift of being open to this support.

Step 5: Release the outcome and trust in the guidance!

When you let go of your plans and trust in a plan that is much greater than yours, you surrender. You can then feel your guides leading you to the next right action. This is what it means to take spiritually aligned action.

Releasing the outcome is a must to truly be in co-creation with your spirit guides, your evolution team, and your higher self.

Step 6: Trust in your own intuition and psychic abilities!

Believe in yourself. Believe in your ability to call in your guides and your spiritual evolution team. Know that you can connect to these guides and will feel their support. Believe that you have an infinite energy of love that is always within you and around you, supporting you and guiding you.

The more that you trust in your own abilities and Magick, the more you will be able to hear, see and follow the guidance of your team. Allowing this connection in your life is the greatest gift you can give to yourself. You will feel supported and they will assist you in supporting others. They will support you to continue shining your light brightly in this world.

Once you invite in your spiritual evolution team, there are many ways you may experience their presence.

SPARKS AND FLASHES

Sparks of light are another way you can tell your spirit guides and team are around you. I often see little sparks of light and colour or flashes at the corners of my vision, particularly when I have spoken with my team and asked for their assistance. All of these confirm for me that they have heard my requests.

THROUGH WRITING

You can call on your team of guides through meditation, even a guided meditation to meet your guides can help, and then proceeding your meditation you can free-write or auto-write. This allows the voice of your guides to work through you at a deeper level.

INNER KNOWING

You may experience them as an inner knowing, a voice within. You may be able to audibly hear the voice of your spirit guide(s), or you may even be able to see them or feel them or all three.

SYNCHRONICITY

Seeing numbers on a clock, like 11:11 or 4:44 for example, or seeing the same cars or numbers on a licence plate, seeing symbols or the same word repeated, all of these are synchronicities and all are a confirmation for you. Synchronicity shows up to let you know you are in alignment and your spiritual team and angels are near.

BOOKS FALLING OFF THE SHELF, CARDS FLYING OUT OF YOUR ORACLE DECK OR THINGS MOVING AROUND.

When books fall off the shelf, or cards fly out of your oracle deck, things move around, go missing mysteriously, or jump out at you, know it is your spirit guides attempting to get your attention. Look for the message or the sign that is being offered to you.

SIGNS

Sometimes you may see signs like butterflies or feathers, flickering lights, rainbows, or orbs. You may even have sensations like chills or tingling on the skin. I often feel the sensation of something touching my head (crown chakra) as the angels and spirits gather around. You could hear voices, smell a particular scent, feel warmth, love and joy or find coins or items that remind you of a person in spirit.

You can even ask for a particular sign if you want to be sure. Just make sure it is a simple sign and you are not asking for spirit to jump through hoops; it takes a lot of energy from spirit to be able to give you a sign so don't make it too convoluted.

MEDITATION

Another great way to get clear is to meditate on it. This ancient practice will help you to get into an altered consciousness, gain more awareness, and achieve more peace. Meditation helps in connecting into the subconscious mind and into the creative energy. Try this simple daily guidance meditation to get more connected.

Start by doing a 10 to 15 minute meditation, relaxing into and allow your spirit to speak through you.

Visualise the things you love, the experiences you would like to have and how that feels.

Daily Guidance Meditation

Close your eyes and take deep breaths. Breathing in through the nose and exhaling through the mouth. Keep focused on your breath and feel it moving through your body, in and out.

Feel your muscles relaxing. See a beautiful golden white light streaming down from above as it now enters the top of your head (your crown chakra). You can now see the light moving through your body and as it does you feel your whole body surrendering and relaxing.

Allow any mind chatter to now just drift away or place it in a lock box to deal with later. Allow any sounds you hear to become a part of your meditation. Give yourself permission to experience this meditation knowing that whatever you experience is in perfect order and harmony with your destiny.

Imagine now that you are walking along a shimmering golden pathway. You feel at peace and are relaxed. As you walk along, up ahead you see a door at the end of the path. It is a lime green colour and it feels inviting. This lime green door is the door to your heart and your soul and as you walk up to the door, you place your hand on the door handle. You feel a tingle of excitement as you open the door and walk through.

Stepping through the door, the most magical space appears. This is your sanctuary. A place you can visit anytime you like. It feels safe here. Protected.

Notice where this safe space exists in your body.

The sanctuary is filled with the most beautiful garden and trees and there is a beautiful body of water in the centre of this space. It is inviting as you walk over you look at your reflection in the body of water. The water sparkles and as you look at your reflection you see that this is a reflection into your soul. An opportunity to connect deeply with your higher self and receive guidance, love, and support.

Start by asking for guidance and by being open to the insights you receive. Set the intention to connect with your spirit and let your inner voice speak to you. You can ask for clarity, your next step, which path is best and for help in making decisions.

Just allow any information to flow through into your awareness now.

Everything is as it should be. Spend as long as you like here deeply connected with yourself and your higher guidance.

When you are ready simply say thank you to your soul for sharing and look once more at your reflection and say – I love you (your name) and I will visit again soon.

As you walk away from the body of water, you take in the beauty that surrounds you. You walk back towards the lime green door and again place your hand on the door handle as you bid farewell to your sanctuary and promise to return soon. As you step through the door and back onto the golden pathway you feel the warmth of the sun on your cheeks, the wind in your hair and you feel your body returning to the present moment.

You wiggle your toes and open your eyes and you are now back in the room with full memory and awareness of your experience.

Once you have finished the meditation come back to your journal and allow your higher self to speak to you and come through your writing. You will have full memory of your connection with your higher self.

Here are some prompts to help get you started. Focus on what brings you joy, love, happiness, and peace.

What do you love doing?

How do you want to feel?

What lights you up and sets your soul on fire?

What action do you need to take to make this happen?

Who do you need to be to live your best life?

What is your divine soul mission?

Note down any ideas, insights, thoughts, or revelations that come up during this process. Just allow yourself to be guided, do not overthink it. Look through your insights and circle the ones that feel the most authentic for you. Make a list of your 4 most authentic and the clarity you received around them.

**Please note: this meditation can be done with or without the journal exercise, but I always find it helpful to note down the things I remember straight after meditation whilst it is still at the forefront of my waking consciousness and fresh in my mind.

There are many ways to get clear on what it is you really want. The practices above I have tried and tested and have found to be the most profound and cathartic. They can be used daily for faster results and will assist you to get really clear on what really sets your heart and soul on fire.

So now you are clear on what you want to create in your life, the next step is to clear what is standing in the way of you manifesting your desires.

> *WITCH* **tip:**
>
> You can record this meditation in your own voice and listen back to it with headphones on so as not to disrupt the flow. Or if you would like my recording please email me.
>
> karen@karenstevens.com.au

The next chapter will assist you to purge and let go of all those old self-sabotaging behaviours and limiting beliefs that have been programmed in your DNA, your mind, and your consciousness.

CHOOSE YOU

YOU ARE BEING ASKED TO CHOOSE TO LET GO OF YOUR NEGATIVE THOUGHTS AND SELF-TALK NOW.

AND ALLOW MORE SPACE FOR POSITIVE EXPERIENCES TO BE ATTRACTED INTO YOUR LIFE.

AFFIRMATION:

I CHOOSE TO LET GO OF NEGATIVE THOUGHTS

CHAPTER 6

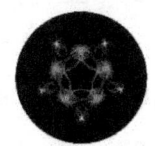

Declutter your mind. Clearing limiting beliefs and self-sabotage.

Clearing limiting beliefs and the self-sabotages that come with them is a priority when it comes to Magick. As you clear your old limiting belief systems, you begin to see that you are the only one standing in the way of your success, fulfillment, and joy and you open your energy field to unlimited possibility and miracles. This part of the journey is one of the most Magickal because it is where you get to reprogram your DNA.

Let me explain a little about your DNA and how it can store much more than just your physical traits.

Every organism on Earth contains the molecular instructions for life, called deoxyribonucleic acid or DNA. These molecular instructions can be altered using epigenetics, energy and light. DNA is programmable and you pass on far more to your children than scientists once thought. We all know for sure that we inherit our physical traits like hair colour, eye colour, height, hereditary disease/conditions etc; but did you know that we also pass on emotions, beliefs, fear, trauma, memories and more.

DNA is not solely a molecular structure; it is stored as a code made up of four chemical bases – Adenine, Guanine, Cytosine and Thymine, and makes up the components of our body. Research is now demonstrating that it is also a transmitter of signals that carry information. This has always fascinated me as not only do I have a deep spiritual connection; I have a deep desire for scientific discovery and answers. And science is catching up to what we inherently know spiritually.

DNA science shows us that ordinary tissue can be re-organized by energetic fields into other things and that DNA can be energetically transferred. This has been proven time and time again by science.

There is a photonic aspect to DNA. A single photon can store the genetic signature of DNA then that DNA can be remotely transferred by light. This is why energy healing (the use of intention, consciousness, will and frequency) is so powerful and why it is the way of our future. Our DNA can be reprogrammed and repaired using energy; working with intention (consciousness).

The consciousness frequencies involved interact with the DNA which transmits the information for chemical reactions thus restoring cell functioning and enabling us to change generational patterns and genetic predispositions.

This is happening in our world consistently – just look at the influence media can have on the masses, creating fear, stress, and anxiety. This is a chemical reaction happening within your body directly affecting your nervous system, your immune system, and your DNA. It can lead to permanent DNA damage and a repeating of the symptoms or illness that this chemical reaction created.

In other words our DNA can be programmed, and if programmed negatively or with fear, it can keep us stuck in limiting beliefs, negative behaviours, patterns, loops and illness.

Knowing that DNA could be reprogrammed was an exciting truth for a woman like me. I saw the possibilities in this and set about learning as much as I could and created ways in which I could transform and create rapid change for my clients. I had suffered debilitating trauma in my life and after a lot of trial and error, I developed the techniques I use today with my private clients who have also suffered immense traumas in their lives.

Upgrading your DNA is simply the beginning. It will allow a clear path to fully activate your innate Magickal and spiritual gifts and steps you into the powerful Goddess you divinely are.

You cannot be in your full power until you start replacing the things that are blocking your success. As I said earlier in this guide, this is a journey, a process back to self and as you follow along you will find your awareness grows, your fear and stress lessens, and you begin to feel more love for yourself and more trust in your intuition. It is the all exciting journey back to YOU.

So, let us start on decluttering your mind, banishing those limiting beliefs and saying farewell to self-sabotage for good.

DECLITTERING YOUR MIND

The first step you need to take is to start decluttering the mind. This is a process for sure. It will not happen overnight, but it will happen. For some of us it can be like cleaning out a hoarder's paradise, so it will happen a little more slowly. But please do not fret, it will happen and if you continue to use the invocations, it will happen far more easily and faster than your previous attempts.

Begin by making the conscious mind decision that no matter what, you are determined, and will not give up on yourself.

Your subconscious mind works like a computerized filing system, it stores and receives data that it has filed from your experiences, thoughts, and feelings. Your subconscious mind ensures you respond in the way you have been programmed (the sum of your experiences and beliefs). Its function is to make sure everything you say and do fits a pattern consistent with your self-concept, your master program. Your subconscious mind is subjective and does not think or reason independently; it obeys the commands it receives from your conscious mind. Your subconscious mind ensures your behaviours match patterns consistent with your emotions.

So knowing that you are simply responding to your "master program" can make the process more digestible, as you are work towards upgrading that master program to allow more of what you truly desire into your life.

COMMIT TO YOU

The powerful action of committing to yourself can sometimes be the difference between reaching your desires or giving up on yourself. Use the following commitment statement to hold yourself accountable, the ultimate act of self-love – the promise that you will not give up on YOU!

Self-commitment accountability contract

I (your name and date) am making a commitment to myself to free myself from the invisible walls I have built around myself. I will now choose love over fear and have compassion for myself in every area of my life. I am making a commitment to change, to empowerment and to loving myself fully without judgement, knowing that I am worthy and deserving of every one of my heart's desires.

Today I choose to go after my dreams and create a life I love, full of joy, peace, and contentment.

I promise myself I will stay focused and every day I will take inspired action, big or small, to help me achieve my dreams. I will continue even when it seems like it will not happen, or others say I cannot. I will not give up. Ever. I am 100% committed to embracing my inner WITCH (Woman in Total Control of Herself) and claiming my Divine Birthright.

Date: _____ Signed: _____

Date: _____ Witnessed: _____

REFRAMING AND REPROGRAMMING

Begin reprogramming by reframing. Every time a negative thought pops into your mind, it is time to silence that "Negative Nancy" and instantly reframe the thought. For example: every time the thought that I cannot do something pops into my mind, I pause, and I say to myself; that is not true, I can and will do it, just watch me.

I like to have a healthy banter with myself and challenge myself to overcome the thought that my "Krazy Karen" (that's what I like to call my Negative Nancy – you can name yours too, it makes it far more relevant when you are speaking to your negative ego counterpart) has tried to sabotage me with. This is a part of your mind health. Keeping your mind under the guidance of your heart.

The mind is an over achiever. It likes to overthink things, especially the negative things.

Experts estimate that the mind thinks between 60,000 – 80,000 thoughts a day. That is an average of 2500 – 3,300 thoughts per hour. That is incredible. Just imagine if just 50% of those thoughts were negative, that would have a HUGE impact on the way you think and feel about yourself, and will most definitely be a contributing factor into what you are or are not bringing into your life.

Reframing is just another way to be kind and compassionate to yourself. Every time I catch myself in the negative pattern, I ask this very simple question – is this how love would respond?

To slow the mind down continue with your daily practice of meditation and continue reframing. It takes an average of 28 days to change a neural pathway so keep practicing daily and before long you will notice that your thoughts are beginning to transform and you are becoming a whole lot more compassionate towards yourself.

I always love to use some Magick to help you along with this process. I have developed a heart-mind connection activation to energetically assist you to surrender control to your heart and reprogram the master program to a more positive version.

This is especially good for those of you that get really stuck in the negative or are stuck in the hustle of trying to make things happen. Surrendering the control from your mind to your heart is allowing your soul to take charge, handing control over to your Divine Feminine (your intuition) and allowing the heart to guide you, and once the guidance is given then handing that over to the Divine Masculine (the mind) to action the guidance. This is being in flow. This is authenticity. The feeling of total peace and mastery.

So please, join with me in the following activation.

THE HEART-MIND CONNECT- THE MARRIAGE OF THE DIVINE FEMININE AND DIVINE MASCULINE.

Before you begin, if you haven't already, open your sacred space and ensure you are somewhere you will not be disturbed. As always, feel free to light some candles, play soft, soothing music, hold or place crystals around you, whatever feels right, allow yourself to be guided by your own intuition.

The purpose of setting the scene is to assist you to drop into a space that you will relax enough to allow your higher self to take control. If you find it difficult to relax, invite your spirit to step forward and take charge of your body.

Now take some deep breaths before you start, just centring your energy, and as you exhale let go of any tension, stress or negative thoughts or emotions that are lingering.

Imagine, feel, or perceive a brilliant white light now streaming down through the top of your head (your crown chakra) and this luscious liquid light is now filling your entire body with pure white light. Your body and soul are now beaming with unconditional love and abundance!

Please read this out loud:

"Dearest Divine,

I request the blessing of Divine Light and manifestations of eternal love from every vibration of the Cosmic Mind to now assist me to activate my heart mind connection, bringing my Divine Feminine and Divine Masculine into unity and harmony now.

I command the full removal of:

- The Seven Houses of Ego.

- All Victim-victimizer programs.

- All negative beliefs, cords, contracts, curses, or conditions blocking the reconnection of the heart-mind.

- All 2D walls of separation of guilt, shame, unworthiness, self-doubt, lack of trust, betrayal, abandonment, anger, rage, fear, entrapment, and enslavement.

- All cellular memory of trauma or abuse.

- All predator forces and negative energies or entities.

- Blockages in the Pericardium Shield.

To allow the activation and purification of my heart-mind connection by unlocking the words of power: Arom Nahrea - Keli, Lekab, Lehah, Sael, Vaho, Doni, Aumem, Mabeh, Aiau - Arom Nahrea.

I now command full activation of:

- My heart-brain complex.

- The Crystal Heart.

- My Human 12 Tree Grid – the tree of life.

- Harmony and balance between my Divine Feminine and Divine Masculine.

- My 12 DNA strands and Aurora Body.

- Self-Compassion and Kindness. "

Now focus your attention on your heart space. Pull your awareness into this space. And as you do so, visualize, sense, or perceive a golden cord coming from this heart space. At the end of the cord is a plug and you see this cord now travel up towards your mind (your third eye chakra) and watch as this plug connects into this space and forms a circuit of continuous glowing, loving energy flowing in harmony between your heart and your mind.

Your mind feels clear and you feel deeply connected, peaceful, serene, and calm.

Your heart and mind are relaying messages of love and connection and you feel a wave of relief and calmness washing over your entire body. It is now safe for your heart and soul to be heard, witnessed, respected, and honoured by your mind.

This feels like a coming home for your soul and you feel powerful as your energy is aligned and in flow.

You surrender fully into this feeling and as you do you say out loud:

"I now anchor lock and seal this heart mind connection throughout my hologram, anchor lock and seal through my subconscious, my DNA and the time matrix.

And so, it is.

Thank you, thank you, thank you Divine".

SELF-SABOTAGE

Self-sabotage is when you actively or passively take steps to prevent yourself from reaching your goals and your full potential. This behaviour can affect nearly every aspect of your life; relationships, career, finances, or personal goals like weight loss or exercising. Self-sabotage is very common, and it is an incredibly frustrating cycle of behaviour that will lower your self-confidence and leave you feeling stuck.

Some Common Self-Sabotage Behaviours

- Procrastination.
- You overthink or delay taking action.
- Give up easily or too soon.
- Inability to control emotions.
- Do not assert yourself or your preferences.
- Staying in abusive relationships.
- Negative self-talk.
- Avoid conflict.
- Trust issues.
- Prone to self-doubt and imposter syndrome.
- Depression.
- Frozen in fear.
- Lack of self-control.
- Attracting continual 'crisis' ort chaos.
- Addictive behaviours/co-dependency.
- Failure to reflect on and learn from mistakes.
- Weight loss then gain again.
- Worrying excessively.

WHY DO WE SELF-SABOTAGE?

Most self-sabotage comes from a space of fear and lack and is a behaviour we partake in instead of facing up to what is really going on. Self-sabotage is an emotional pay off with yourself.

Not taking responsibility or placing the blame somewhere else.

When you believe that you are not going to do well or will fail you will begin behaving in a manner that ensures you will fail. When you think things like "I won't get that job anyway" you are displacing your responsibility in achieving success. So, you do not fully prepare for the interview and when you do not get the job you can justify not preparing as you have already accepted that you will not succeed. Instead you will transfer the blame to someone or something else.

Lack of self-worth

If you do not believe in yourself, you cannot achieve your goals. A feeling of unworthiness will leave you feeling less confident, coupled with the constant reminders of the mind chatter telling you that you are not smart enough, qualified enough, or good enough to have what you want, you will act accordingly to what is playing over in your mind. The way you speak to yourself matters and directly

affects how you present to the world. When you lack confidence, you will continue to do things that stop you from achieving your fullest potential.

Wanting to control your life.

You feel better when you feel like you are in control. By accepting the negative outcome ahead of time, you feel that you are in control even though it is not the outcome your truly desire. You are in effect controlling your failure in the process of trying to control all outcomes.

Fearing success.

That old chestnut – imposter syndrome. When you lack self-confidence you can worry and stress that you are not qualified enough, not trained enough, do not have enough wisdom or are not prepared enough and this ultimately will lead to you being exposed as a fraud. Your fear of success leads you to engage in behaviour that will limit the success you could achieve. As you get close to success, your fear sets in and you take a step back in fear of not being good enough.

Fear of failure.

The fear that you are not good enough plays a role in the fear of failure also. This is the most overwhelming reason why you continue to self-sabotage. Feeling that your best will never be good enough, you give yourself reasons as to why you failed, rather than facing the reality of giving it your all and still not succeeding.

In all these scenarios it is the subconscious mind in operation keeping you safe, comfortable, and running the program in the background – that master program. Your subconscious mind will continue to run the master belief program to deliver the outcomes you believe to be true for you.

Are you ready to clear self-sabotage from your life?

The following clearing and activation will assist you in dissolving those self-sabotage behaviours.

CLEARING THE EMOTIONAL PAY OFF TO SELF-SABOTAGE

Before you begin, if you have not already, open your sacred space and ensure you are somewhere you will not be disturbed. As always, feel free to light some candles, play soft, soothing music, hold or place crystals around you, whatever feels right, allow yourself to be guided by your own intuition.

The purpose of setting the scene is to assist you to drop into a space that you will relax enough to allow your higher self to take control. If you find it difficult to relax, invite your spirit to step forward and take charge of your body.

Now take some deep breaths before you start, just centring your energy, and as you exhale let go of any tension, stress or negative thoughts or emotions that are lingering.

Imagine, feel, or perceive a brilliant white light now streaming down through the top of your head (your crown chakra) and this luscious liquid light is now filling your entire body with pure white light. This light will assist you in releasing these old behaviours and patterns and dissolve them into liquid light.

Please read aloud with intention:

"Dearest Divine Loving Source,

Please bless me with your Divine Grace and assist me to safely release all self-sabotage behaviours and emotional payoffs so I may let go of and release, clear, dissolve and disconnect all negative attachments, cords, ties and connections to these behaviours."

Focus again on this luscious liquid light that is flowing down through your crown chakra and see yourself completely bathed in this light as it enters ever cell of your body.

As you stand in this light you witness the reasons for your self-sabotaging behaviour, and you realize that these behaviours are no longer necessary. You choose to let them go and forgive yourself. You send love to yourself and choose now to move forward leaving behind these negative emotions and behaviours.

You feel the healing light now moving through every cell of your being as your DNA is being upgraded and purified and reprogrammed with strength, courage and loving life force energy.

Connect with your Divine essence now and the feeling of love and acceptance as you choose to embrace all that you are.

Say aloud:

"I am free of these self-sabotaging behaviours and the need to keep playing small, I accept my gifts and step into my full power. I love the woman I am and the woman I am becoming.

Thank you, thank you, thank you.

And so, it is".

> **WITCH tip:**
>
> Essential oils to use for this release are: Cedarwood, Frankincense or Bergamot.
>
> Crystals to use for this release are: Smoky Quartz.

BANISHING LIMITING NEGATIVE BELIEFS

There are so many things you have been taught to believe that oppose the all-powerful Laws of the Universe. True power comes when you are in flow, in alignment with your own frequency and the frequency of the Universe. Power lies in letting go of resistance and allowing the flow of the Universe to fill and become one with you.

Your core beliefs, the basic beliefs that you have about yourself, other people and the world around you, are those things that you hold deep down as absolute truth, underneath all of your surface thoughts. Your core beliefs really determine how you perceive and interpret this world. These beliefs sit in the subconscious mind, and when something happens, your subconscious opens and consults the core belief in the master program. The belief that is most likely to keep you safe and defend you against this world. As you will have experienced, these core beliefs are dominant and convincing, and they are full of persuasion and conviction.

You simply accept your core beliefs as truth without question. These beliefs are seated deep within your mind and you live your life around these beliefs without thinking about them, questioning or even being aware of them.

Core beliefs are an important level of measurement because they determine to what degree you see yourself as worthy, safe, competent, powerful, or loved. Your negative beliefs can have deadly consequences to your self-acceptance and your self-esteem. Your core beliefs have a huge influence on your sense of belonging, and how you are viewed and treated by others. What you feel you are worthy of and what you deserve. Or even what you think you can achieve in this lifetime.

Some of these beliefs come from childhood programming. Your parent's beliefs are communicated to you through words and actions. Therefore, your parent's beliefs shape what you believe to be true. So, the beliefs that you receive in childhood, condition, and program you, and are critical, because the child's mind is like a sponge. It shapes what you become and what you believe about yourself and this world.

These negative beliefs that exist in your subconscious mind are consistently attracting the experiences to you that prove that they exist and prove to you that they are true. But these beliefs are false beliefs, because if you look around, not everyone believes the same thing. And not everyone attracts the same thing. As children, your belief system, self-esteem is derived by the way that you are treated. This includes all your experiences, not just those with your parents and siblings, but those experiences within your schooling, your friend circles and from experiences with social media or media in general. This results in having a fixed opinion of yourself as an adult. Your past experiences confirm your belief systems now.

You have many belief systems, therefore it is important that you identify and connect with those belief systems so that you can reprogram them.

For example, in my vintage, the cliché was – Children should be seen and not heard. The result of this was varying negative beliefs – I am not valued, my opinion does not count, my voice does not matter, I am worthless, etc. These negative beliefs have real time reactions. Many children who experienced this, struggle with speaking up for themselves or speaking their truth. They have trouble with authority or that they need to be submissive, or a people pleaser to be liked or valued. The implications are endless and are based on the negative belief you take into the subconscious as your truth.

When looking at relationships, negative beliefs, such as I am not good enough, can cause you to lose confidence in yourself and your ability to get what you want, resulting in settling for second best. You just need to look at the state of relationships in the 21st century to know that the belief of; "I am not good enough" is a very common theme. Relationship breakdowns, domestic violence, and suicide are just a few of the consequences of this negative belief and pattern. Many people just do not feel worthy, at the very core level. This is a core belief system.

Here are some other belief systems that are derived from different types of clichés as well.

For example:

Money does not grow on trees.

Money's very hard to come by.

You cannot have everything you want.

Get your head out of the clouds. You are such a dreamer.

You are a black sheep.

You cannot be spiritual and rich.

I cannot afford it.

I do not have enough.

I am bad.

I cannot do anything right.

I am unlovable.

People are untrustworthy.

The world is dangerous, not safe.

LETS' LOOK AT SOME OF THE NEGATIVE BELIEF SYSTEMS

Almost all negative core beliefs are connected to the broader feeling of low self-worth or the feeling of not being enough. But we are going to delve deeper than that and zero in on more precise core beliefs that will help you free yourself from the pattern and the cycle.

This is where your muscle testing skills will get a workout.

Below is a list of negative beliefs, patterns, and systems that you may have running in your master program. Next to them is the positive that you will be replacing and reprogramming.

They describe your core issue and those two or three words can set up a negative pattern that you will bond to and repeat throughout your life, until you can release them and balance them with a positive program.

Negative Belief System Patterns	Positive Reprogram
1. Life – Life is hard, Life is not meant to be easy, I don't deserve to live, I am tired of living.	Life is happening for me and I am open to experiencing all the joy life brings towards me.
2. Peace – There will never be world peace, I can't get any peace, I am always stressed.	Peace resides within me and I feel a deep level of peace in my heart now.

3. Family – Family first, Blood is thicker than water, I must follow in my family's footsteps.	I am a sovereign being and I choose to surround myself with people who love and nourish me.
4. Males- Men are aggressive, Men are stronger, Men cannot be trusted. Men are superior.	The men I encounter in my life are loving, kind and compassionate and are my equal.
5. Females – Women are weak, Women are bitchy, Women are cruel, women are jealous.	The women I encounter in my life are supportive, kind and loving. We empower one another.
6. Harmony – I am a mess, I can't get it together, I can't find anything, My life is chaotic.	I am balanced and all my energy centres are aligned and harmonious and this is reflected back to me in my life now.
7. Unwelcome – I don't belong, I don't fit in, I am lost, I am alone, I am unwanted.	I am welcomed everywhere I go, and I feel a deep sense of being home. I belong.
8. Bad – I'm no good, it's my fault, I am hopeless, I am imperfect, I don't deserve anything.	I am perfect just as I am. I am loving, kind and have a heart full of love.

9. Receiving – I don't deserve good things in my life, I don't exist, I am not good enough.	I am enough and I welcome in and receive abundance in my life on every level now.
10. Loyalty – I can't commit, I'm disposable, I always come second, Nobody cares about me.	I am committed to the relationship I have with myself and am loyal to my heart. I am loved and cared for by the Universe.
11. Boundaries – I can't control anything, I can't change, I am powerless, I am inferior.	I set clear boundaries to support my wellbeing and I uphold these boundaries without exception.
12. Learning – Learning is hard, You can't teach an old dog new tricks, I was always bad at school.	I learn things easily and can tap into the deep reservoir of knowledge and wisdom I have within my own spirit.
13. Change – Change is scary, I can't change, Change is too hard, Nothing ever changes.	I embrace change with an open heart as I step into the woman I choose to be.
14. Success – Nothing works for me, I always get it wrong, I am a failure, I can't make it work.	I am a success, in fact everything I do now is successful as I choose to commit to seeing things through and never giving up on myself.

15. Stupid – I am stupid, I am slow, I never get it right, I am a loser, I am a failure.	I am aware and astute, and I choose to succeed in my life.
16. Control – I can't control anything, Others manipulate & control me, I must control my life.	I allow the flow of the Universe to move through me as I surrender and allow my frequency to align with the Universal frequency of Love.
17. Spirituality/Religion – I have no hope, I must sacrifice myself to be saved, I have lost my spirit.	I connect deeply within my own soul and divinity whilst knowing I am always connected with Source energy and the Oneness of all.
18. Identity – I am lost, I am alone, I don't know who I am, I don't matter, I am no-one.	I am a powerful woman filled with purpose and passion and love. I am a Goddess and I honour this in myself now.
19. Health – I am always ill, I can't get better, My health is failing, I am scared of death.	I choose optimal health for my entire body and energy system. I have everything I need within to ensure I feel healthy and well.

20. Self-Healing – I am unfixable, I am doomed, I have a mental problem, I cannot be healed.	I have everything I need within to heal my entire energy system. I need only to call on my higher self to lead the way.
21. Wholeness – I am not whole, I am broken, I have lost my spirit, I am empty, I am evil.	I am whole and I choose to reconnect with all of my 617 living soul facets as I connect deeply in with all that I am.
22. Security – I'm not safe, I'm vulnerable, I'm unprotected, I'm afraid, Nobody will protect me.	I am safe and fully supported by the Universe and Divine Source continuously. I have my own energy protection system that is fully activated.
23. Relationships – I am not enough, I need people to like me, Who would want me anyway?	I am loved, adored, and cherished and I only attract loving, nurturing & divinely blessed relationships to myself from this moment forwards.
24. Self-Worth – I am flawed, I am not enough, I am worthless, I have no value, I'm nothing.	I know on every level of my being that I am enough, I am valued and worthy of all the abundance the Universe has to offer me.

25. Love – I don't deserve to be loved, Nobody loves me, I am jealous, Love hurts.	I am love. I come from love and I will return to love. I feel unconditional love for myself and others now as I allow my frequency to align with love.
26. Freedom – I am trapped, I have too many responsibilities, I can never be free.	I am free on every level of my being. I allow my soul to expand and flourish knowing I am completely sovereign now.
27. Power – Power is evil, I am powerless, I am overpowered, I am disempowered, I am weak.	I choose to connect to my inner power as this is my greatest gift to myself. I am empowered and I inspire other women to claim their power.
28. Career – I'm not experienced, I'm scared of being turned down, I'm scared of failing.	I easily attract the position that best reflects my true divine purpose and mission on this Earth and in doing so I am happy and successful.
29. The Future – My future looks bleak, I am sacred of the future, I'm scared of the unknown.	I look forward to my future and know that I have the power to create anything I desire as I step into the co- creator and manifester that I am.

30. Abundance – There is not enough to go around, I am not enough, I am not deserving.	I live in an abundant Universe and I am made of this very same abundance. I am enough on every level of my being.
31. Wealth/Prosperity – Money is the root of all evil, money doesn't grow on trees, Money is hard to come by, I must work hard for money.	I love money and money loves me. I attract money into my life with ease knowing that there is a surplus for all.
32. Fear – Fear of failure, Fear of living, Fear of dying, I don't feel safe, I am not supported.	I am love, I radiate and vibrate love into the Universe. I am always 100% supported by the Universe and I am always safe and secure.

Do any of these resonate?

You are now going to look at these more closely and begin to release them and reprogram your beliefs using a Magickal formula I use with my private clients.

This is all a part of you connecting to your inner W.I.T.C.H (Woman in Total Control of Herself).

WITCH

Step 1: Muscle Test.

Start by muscle testing the list on the left-hand side that is numbered. I hope you have been practicing your muscle testing skills in your day to day life so you will be a little more comfortable with the process. For those that may already read or feel energy, or perhaps can intuit you can use your own method of connecting to the number that will correlate to your negative belief and pattern.

Muscle testing, I want you to now choose a number from the list. The easiest way to do this, as there are a lot of numbers, is to ask the following as you are testing.

Is the number between 1 and 10? Yes/No

Is the number between 11 and 21? Yes/No

Is the number between 22 and 32? Yes/No

So, if for example you answered yes to: Is the number between 11 and 21, you would then go on further to drill down on the number. You could say: Is the number between 11 and 16? Yes/No and if the answer is no you will know it is between 17 and 21, so you could begin to muscle test each number between 17 and 21 until you get the yes answer that relates to the number of your negative belief.

This may seem overwhelming at first, but I can assure you with more practice this will become automatic and a fast way to drill down on your negative belief and pattern. I rarely use muscle-testing anymore as my intuition will give me the number instantly that I need to work with. So as much as this is a clearing and reprogramming it is also a practice that will build your intuition fast.

OK, so now you have your number. Let us say for example sake this number is 20.

You will now look at the negative belief and pattern and see how this resonates to you. How does this show up for you in your life? Just bring your awareness to it, do not stress about it as you are going to release it and reprogram the belief with the positive version.

Negative Belief Pattern 20 is Self-Healing – I am unfixable, I am doomed, I have a mental problem, I cannot be healed.

The positive to reprogram with is - I have everything I need within to heal my entire energy system. I need only to call on my higher self to lead the way.

The next part is the fun part where you will reprogram your own DNA.

Please use the following reprogramming command to do this.

BELIEF REPROGRAMMING

Before you begin, if you have not already, open your sacred space and ensure you are somewhere you will not be disturbed. Make sure you are comfortable, take a few deep breaths as you centre your energy into your heart space as you connect within.

Say aloud:

"I call upon my Divine Loving Source, my spiritual evolution team, and all enlightened beings of love and above, to now assist me to reprogram my DNA.

I command access to Creator of All's Pure Divine Healing energy for support, access to all levels of advanced consciousness, dimensions, and timelines now to remove and cancel the negative belief pattern of .... (list the negative belief) running in my master program in my subconscious mind and DNA".

Sensing brilliant white, cleansing, and healing light now encasing your entire being as it streams down through your crown chakra. The light is now drawing out this negative belief program and pattern from your entire energy system. Your spiritual team and angels are there to give you the healing that you need. You can feel this old negative program, including any fear, denial or stress associated with the program being dissolved in the light. Your body and energy system feels lighter and you feel the burden being lifted from you now.

New signals of love, happiness and joy are being created for you to download the new program and positive belief.

Say aloud:

"I now activate the new positive belief and program... (insert the positive program from the opposite side of the old belief) and anchor lock and seal this new program throughout my hologram, anchor lock and seal through my subconscious, my DNA and the time matrix.

I now activate the power sources of the 10 Attributes of God and the Universal Tree of Life throughout my entire energy system.

With gratitude, I confirm the upgrade of my master program.

And so it is".

Most of us have more than one negative belief system or pattern running in our master program so you can use this process as often as you require. Reprogramming the positive has the exponential effect of speeding up the process of connecting to the W.I.T.C.H within. I am always about fast tracking and each command, invocation or spell I create is created with maximum impact to really help you fast track your way into sovereignty and living and being in your full power, aligning with the frequency of the Universe, to live your best life- now!

Remember: With each powerful invocation, you are literally changing at a cellular, molecular, DNA level and that everything must follow from the metaphysical and emotional resolution to the physical body. Choose to embrace any momentary discomfort knowing that it will pass, and the sun will come out again. Choose to let it go.

Always ensure you are compassionate and kind towards yourself as some emotions may come up to be released in the physical world. Ensure you have plenty of filtered water, and rest as often as you can. Your body is upgrading through many dimensions of your existence and your cells are working hard, understanding this will help you in this process.

CHOOSE YOU

YOU ARE BEING ASKED TO CHOOSE TO RELEASE ALL PAST LIFE KARMA AFFECTING YOUR GROWTH.

LET GO OF ALL CURSES DIRECTED AT YOU OR TRANSFERRED TO YOU IN THIS LIFETIME. RELEASE ALL CORDS AND TIES THAT NO LONGER SERVE YOUR HIGHEST GOOD.

CHOOSE TO RELEASE ALL CELLULAR MEMORIES AFFECTING YOUR GROWTH.

AFFIRMATION:

I CHOOSE TO ACCEPT MY KARMA
AND RELEASE IT THROUGH FORGIVENESS

CHAPTER 7

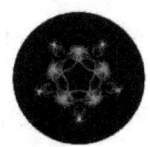

Curses, Psychic Attacks and Karma.

This is one of my favourite topics of interest because it is one that can have the most powerful effect over you, including an equally powerful release that can instantly clear days, months, or years of suffering in just minutes!

Have you ever felt or perhaps even said to yourself – "I am cursed', "I feel attacked" or "I must have a lot of bad karma"? Or have you had days where you feel completely off balance and feel a strong, negative energy surrounding or overcoming you, impacting your thoughts and feelings? These feelings could include distress, fear, insecurity, or a general feeling that something is wrong or about to go wrong. Generally, these feelings get dismissed as "one of those days" as you try to comfort yourself and perhaps treat yourself with some scrumptious yummies whilst binge watching your favourite shows.

What you may not be aware of is that consciously or unconsciously, someone may have formed an intention to harm you. It could be an ex who still harbours ill feelings towards you, or a "frenemy" who is jealous of your looks, success, or financial position. Many times, it can be family who have unresolved, deep seated hate or jealousy. Everyone, like it or not, has some darkness within, the shadow side, that stores those negative feelings and thoughts, and when those unpleasant emotions are not acknowledged and released, the shadow side jumps into the driver's seat.

Let me be clear here; psychic attacks and curses are very real and can have serious effects on the way you are experiencing life and could be holding you back from living the life you desire. There is no need to worry or feel scared at all, you can protect yourself from these negative energies and awareness is the first, most important step.

We will examine these separately and how they can affect you, followed with a powerful release that will reverse the effects of these negative forces.

PSYCHIC ATTACKS

A psychic attack occurs when someone consciously or unconsciously inflicts negative energy upon you. Negative energies occur when negative vibrations (thoughts, feelings etc) are directed from one person to another. This negatively affects the energetic, physical, and emotional bodies of the person who is the receiver. These negative energies can have serious ramifications for you and can cause great physical and mental harm. There are varying forms of psychic attack and most are projected through negative energies, even on a subconscious level. Psychic attacks are like curses although not as binding, considering curses can continue for generations.

There are several ways you can identify if you are being psychically attacked.

1. You may sense or feel you are being watched.
2. Seeing shadows from the corner of your eye.
3. Dreaming about the attacker, or if they are popping into your mind frequently.
4. Unexplained sense of fear.
5. Stabbing feelings in your back or heart.
6. Unpleasant dreams, even nightmares.
7. Feeling like a black cloud of depression suddenly comes over you.
8. Negative thoughts that pop in from nowhere and may not even feel like your own thoughts.

All of these are signs that you could be under psychic attack. There are a few steps you can take to stop the attack and clear the energy.

Step 1: Be Aware.

Acknowledging and recognizing the unusual or strange events happening in your life will help to diminish the effect of the attack. Understanding that this too is just energy can help you to set better boundaries to protect your energy. Afterall, boundaries are all about honing in on your feelings and honouring them, and it is often the times when you are vulnerable or stressed that these boundaries have been relaxed allowing the negative energy to penetrate your personal power and aura.

Step 2: Keep the faith and stay strong.

Emotional stability, keeping strong and having trust and faith in yourself is important to protect against any negative side effects of the attack. Keep positive and do not retaliate. Sending negative energy their way will only serve to lock you into a never-ending energy battle with the attacker.

Step 3: Release the energy.

Use this release to clear the negative effects of the psychic attack.

Negative energy reversal

Before you begin, if you have not already, open your sacred space and ensure you are somewhere you will not be disturbed. As always, feel free to light some candles, play soft, soothing music, hold or place crystals around you, whatever feels right, allow yourself to be guided by your own intuition.

The purpose of setting the scene is to assist you to drop into a space that you will relax enough to allow your higher self to take control. If you find it difficult to relax, invite your spirit to step forward and take charge of your body.

Say aloud:

"I call upon the Great Beloved, The Creator of All that is, and my spiritual evolution team to assist me now to clear and transmute all psychic attack energies, cords and attachments, negative energies and, negative thoughtforms directed towards me from (the name of the person who sent them).

I now sever and release all energetic cords that do not serve my highest good.

I release myself from these cords and ties across all dimensions, within all space and realities and throughout all frameworks of my existence, never to return again.

Please purify, cleanse, and restore my energy field releasing any negative impacts or after affects. Restore and activate my soul life force energy and realign me, mind-body-spirit to balance and harmonize my frequency.

I now seal myself with white and gold purifying light, and I send white light of love and blessings to whom it came from.

Thank you, thank you, thank you.

And so, it is".

Step 4: Clear and protect your energy.

There are many practices for clearing your personal energy. You could use sage smudging sticks, perform an aura cleanse, or house cleanse (see the magical toolbox in Chapter 15 for these), salt baths, or a simple shower to cleanse. Energy protection is like invisible armour protecting your personal energy.

Energy protection

Visualize, sense, or perceive a brilliant white bubble just above your head. As you focus on the bubble it expands further and further out until it encases you within its protective walls.

Now repeat the mantra:

"The Light and Love of the Great Divine, The Creator of All now protects me and watches over me wherever I am. I am loved, safe and am impervious to any frequency less than love whilst protected within this bubble of loving light.

And so, it is".

CURSES

Secular history shows us that curses are real. Curses are mentioned in the Bible over 200 times. There are many types of curses, short and long term, past or present life. A curse is a wish of ill intent, unconsciously or consciously. It is an invocation to bestow harm or injury to the intended target.

Curses can be anything from wishing someone poor health, loss, financial ruin, death, disease, bad luck or can even be for revenge – as in an eye for an eye.

Generational curses are an example of a long-term curse, that are passed along the generational line (stored within the DNA) and are designed to devastate each generation. Known to bring about inconceivable failure in the personal and financial lives of the descendants of the originally cursed person.

Curses can be made either in ceremony, simply by malicious thoughts; thoughts are energy and can be incredibly powerful. Curses can also carry over and continue in future lives and more often than not, you will meet someone from a past life who cursed you then, and the curse will be reactivated in your present life.

There are many types of curses and here are some you may be aware of.

- Black Magic
- Voodoo
- Spells (with negative intent)
- Evil Eye
- Pointing the Bone
- Hexes
- Slavery curses
- Satanic curses
- Satanic rituals
- Taglocks
- Time bombs
- Booby Traps
- Sorcery
- Generational Curses

Some simple signs of being cursed:

1. Inexplicable Illness or multiple injuries.
2. String of bad luck.
3. Random negative thoughts or feelings.
4. Inexplainable repeat loss of job.
5. Missing items or pets.
6. Feelings of being watched.
7. Nightmares.

8. Threatening letters, emails, or messages.
9. Unlucky in love.
10. Repeat illness or disease.
11. Paralysis.
12. Random sharp pains.
13. Feeling a heaviness on your back or shoulders.
14. Generational patterns of illness or misfortune.

All of these are signs that you could be cursed. There are a few steps you can take to dissolve the curse and restore balance to your energy.

Step 1: Be Aware.

As above, awareness is key. Being aware of negative forces allows you to diminish their power. There is great power in truth and shining light on the darkness.

As the late, great Martin Luther King Jr said,

"*Darkness cannot drive out darkness only light can do that. Hate cannot drive out hate only love can do that*".

Keep strong and know that your light shines bright, and the brighter and clearer you keep your light (your frequency) the less the damage from curses will have upon you!

Step 2: Break the Curse.

Use this curse breaking release to clear and break the curse from all lifetimes.

Curse Removal

Before you begin, if you have not already, open your sacred space and ensure you are somewhere you will not be disturbed.

Say aloud:

"I call upon the Great Beloved, The Creator of All that is, and my spiritual evolution team and I ask that the highest vibrations of love and light connect with my highest self now to assist me to break the curse including all cords and attachments, negative energies and, negative thoughtforms directed towards me from (the name of the person who sent them).

I now sever, release, and dissolve all curses across all dimensions, within all space and realities and throughout all frameworks of my existence, never to return again.

I command purification and cleansing to restore my energy field releasing all negative impacts and after affects.

I request full activation of my power sources through the 10 emanations of the Tree of Life and I now seal myself with white and gold purifying light.

I send white light of love and blessings to whom the curse came from.

Thank you, thank you, thank you.

And so, it is".

> **WITCH tip:**
>
> Essential oils to use for this release are: Cedarwood, Frankincense, Vetiver, Lavender, Sandalwood.
>
> Crystals to use for this release are: Kyanite, Pyrite, Black Tourmalinated Quartz.
>
> Archangel that can assist: Archangel Michael.

Step 3: Protection and Blessings.

After a curse release it is important to protect your energy and call in your blessings to replenish any lost energy or draining of energy.

Restore Blessings for Protection

Take a couple of deep breaths, imagine now beautiful, pure, golden light is filling your heart space, filling you with more light, more love, more peace, and more freedom. This light now streams out from your heart and expands outwards and all around you creating a seal completely around you, connecting and strengthening the Etheric, Astral, Mental and Causal layers of your auric field.

Say aloud with intention:

"I now call upon Divine Protection and Divine Blessings to keep me safe and protected.

I accept the blessings of Divine Grace and the restoration of my DNA to my original Divine Bliss Blueprint.

I am ready to leave the past and move forwards in leaps and bounds, into my fullest expression and soul essence.

I accept all that Universe Source has to offer me for freedom, abundance, peace and love and I call in these miracles and blessings now.

Ana Bekoah

We beg thee with the strength and greatness of thy right arm,

Accept your people's song, elevate, and purify them,

Please, powerful one, those who pursue your uniqueness,

Guard them as the pupil of an eye,

Bless them, purify them, have mercy on them,

May your righteousness always reward them,

Powerful and Holy One, in goodness lead your people,

Unique and almighty one, to your people turn,

Who remember your Holiness,

Accept their cries, and hear their pleas,

Oh, knower of mysteries,

Blessed is the name of his noble kingdom forever and ever.

Thank you, thank you, thank you.

And so, it is".

This is both a powerful protection and blessing from the Divine. After any curse removal or negative energy release, I like to balance my energy with blessings and unconditional love. Remember it is the light that will disperse the darkness, always.

WITCH tip:

If you are unsure where the psychic attack or curse has come from you can muscle test anyone you may suspect is the sender. Alternatively, you could meditate and ask for the name or vision of the person who sent it.

KARMA

Let us start by looking at what Karma is.

Karma is a Sanskrit word meaning – action. Karma is often thought of as a punishment for wrong doing, and many are shocked to learn that Karma is simply the sum of your actions in this and previous lifetimes, that records the negative and positive actions you have taken. It relates to the Law of Cause and Effect which states: Every action we take has a reaction or consequence; that every thought, word or action carries energy into the world and affects your reality.

It is important to build positive Karma reserves so that you avoid negative consequences. These are not punishments as such, more of a reactionary response to your actions and thoughts – your energy output. Negative Karma can also serve as part of your spiritual evolution as you face challenges or adversities that require you to learn and grow. The key is to become more self-reflective, and understanding of the lesson as growth, letting go of resistance, so that your path ahead flows more easily and powerfully.

The Universe is not interested in your goal-based achievements, your bank balance or how many houses you own. When you are acting out of kindness, compassion and love you are aligning to your true purpose. This also includes acting in kindness, compassion, and love for yourself as the Universe does not discriminate - nor should you. So, if you have difficulties in being kind to yourself or forgiving yourself or others, you may like to try the below Karma Repair. Releasing Karma can be the breath of fresh air that inspires you to be the best version of yourself.

Karma Repair

Before you begin, if you have not already, open your sacred space and ensure you are somewhere you will not be disturbed.

Say aloud with intention:

"I call upon the powers of The Creator of All that is, the Lords of Karma, and my spiritual evolution team to assist in the cleansing, clearing and transmutation of all negative Karmic imprints in my Akasha.

I call on the Law of Forgiveness. I forgive everyone and everything and I ask forgiveness from everyone and everything. I forgive myself.

I ask to be surrounded with Divine purifying light and call upon the assistance of my protections angels to cleanse my energy on every level.

Dearest Divine, please release from my energy field, all that no longer serves me for my best and highest good, release it into the light and replace it with gratitude, compassion, and joy.

Step me into alignment with my highest Divine Truth.

I request full activation of my power sources through the 10 emanations of the Tree of Life and I now seal myself with white and gold purifying light.

Thank you, thank you, thank you.

And so, it is".

You can follow up this Karma Repair with The Ho'oponopona Prayer of forgiveness to release and balance your Karma and keep it clear.

If you feel that you would like to be able to let go and forgive, not only others, but yourself; the practice of the Ho'oponopono is very powerful and can literally transform your mindset, your mood, or any problems you may be experiencing. You can make amends for past mistakes that are weighing on your consciousness, simply and lovingly.

Ho'oponopono means to make right. Ho'o (to make) and pono (right) with the emphasis on right being repeated. Practice the Ho'oponopono as often as you like. I practice this daily and often chant this in my mind over and over. It is truly powerful and will promote peace within.

The Ho'oponopona Prayer

- I'm sorry
- Please forgive me
- Thank you
- I love you

As you can see this prayer is so simple to remember and use anywhere. Practice it often and keep the peace with your Karma.

Steps to creating positive Karma in your life

1. Gratitude: be grateful for all experiences, both negative and positive.
2. Compassion: act with love for everyone, no matter what they may have done, try to find that space of compassion and understanding.
3. Intention: are your intentions coming from a place of love for self and others?
4. Positive thoughts: keep a check on negative thoughts or feelings as these create angry energy directed at you. Keep your thoughts positive.
5. Forgiveness: this is one of the most challenging, but the most rewarding. Forgiveness of self and others is important in building positive Karmic reserves.

CHOOSE YOU

YOU ARE BEING ASKED TO CHOOSE TO PRIORITIZE YOUR LIFE, YOUR DREAMS AND YOUR GOALS EVERY DAY.

FOCUS ON YOUR INTENTIONS, WISHES AND DREAMS AND TAKE INSPIRED ACTION TOWARDS THEM EVERY SINGLE DAY.

AFFIRMATION:

I CHOOSE TO PRIORITIZE MY LIFE WITH INTENTION.

CHAPTER 8

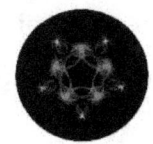

Setting Powerful Intentions.

Your intention is vital. Intention sets the scene for the outcome. It is the calling in of your vision. Intention is powerful when using Magick and creating miracles. Just as you would set a GPS to get you to your destination, setting an intention will steer you to your desired outcome.

Intention also determines whether a spell or invocation has a negative or positive karmic outcome. Your intentions must be set for your best and highest good and must not harm anyone else in the process. Having positive karmic reserves is important for the advancement of your soul's evolution.

HOW DO I SET AN INTENTION?

Everything that happens in the Universe begins with intention. It is the starting point of every dream, goal, or desire. Intention is the creative power that will serve to deliver your needs and desires.

In previous chapters, you have learned ways to get clearer on exactly what you want to create or experience in your life. This is now the time to put that desire into intention.

Look at your priorities first. The focus points that were most important to you when you went through the clarity exercises and meditation.

Look at what you want to show up in your life and how you want to feel. Feeling is very important as it connects the vision into your energy body. What we think and feel becomes reality. This is key in manifesting and aligning our frequency with what we desire.

When writing an intention, it is important to write it in a positive framework. The Universe cannot decipher the negative. So, if you say – I do not want to be in debt for example, the focus is on the debt not that you do not want it. Remember what we focus on grows, what we resist, persists.

Here are some examples of the negative in a positive light.

Transform your dislikes into a powerful request to the Universe and the Universe will respond.

NEGATIVE	POSITIVE
Fear. I am scared.	Trust and freedom. Feeling safe and secure.
In debt.	Financial freedom. Abundance.
Sadness. Depression.	Joy, happiness, contentment.

Stress. Worry.	Peace of mind. Deep inner peace.
Tired. Gives up. Does not care.	Passion for life. Energized Life Force.
Low self-worth.	Self-empowerment, self-love, sovereignty.
Disharmony in relationships.	Nourishing relationships. Nurtured, supported. Harmonious connections
Poor health. Patterns of sabotage – ie: I get sick when I am close to achieving something.	I want to be vibrant and healthy on all levels.

Your intention can be short and to the point or more elaborate describing everything your desire and wish to feel in your life.

Here is an example of a past intention I channelled for a private client. You can see it is elaborate and continuously written in the positive.

"I choose to 100% fully accept and love myself on every level of my being.

I have a strong, clear, continuous connection to myself and my loving Divine Universal source and have complete trust and faith in my feelings and my intuition.

It is 100% safe for me to open my heart and receive in my life on every level. It is safe for me to love and be loved.

I take full responsibility as co-creator in my life, and I now fully embrace, welcome in, and reclaim my personal power.

I attract only frequencies of love and higher to myself now and I am impervious to any frequency less than love.

I nourish my body with food that uplifts me, and my body responds with strength, vitality, and optimal health. I love my body and my body loves me.

I can now enjoy all the abundance, unconditional love, peace, and joy that now flows into my life with ease and with grace.

I have the freedom, the finances, and the confidence to enjoy my life as I choose to, and my children are thriving alongside me.

I am a Divine, confident, connected, and courageous woman.

I love the woman I am and the woman I am becoming.

And so, it is".

As you can see your intention can be detailed. Setting an intention is a powerful way to speak directly to the Universe. You are conjuring your Magick. You are stepping into a world full of possibilities and opportunities. I am here to tell you that WHATEVER YOU WANT in your life; your Divine soulmate, to live your life's purpose with ease and flow, happiness, security, safety, financial wealth, health, abundance, whatever it is; You CAN have ALL of it – you are supposed to, and you deserve it.

NOW IT'S YOUR TURN

The goal of this exercise is to shed light into your heart and soul and clear a path to your dreams. Using your notes from the previous chapter on getting clarity, look at the words, statements and dreams that really stand out to you.

Review each of them and elaborate on them if required then categorize them into areas like, wellness, career, relationships, habits etc. Now it is time to allow your creative self to take over, allow the words to flow onto the paper, or use your journal. Write them down in the most positive version of what you would love to experience or have.

When you are happy with your intention, re-write it so that it is narrative in style. Begin with I, and then write your name, finish the intention with "And so it is" or "Mote it be" or "So be it" - whichever resonates the most with you. Then read your intention aloud, speak from the heart and the Universe will be listening. Feel the words you are speaking and let them flow with the Universal Laws knowing that what you have just spoken is now finding its way to you.

Congratulations, you are on the way to creating Magick and calling in your innermost desires into your life.

INTENTION SETTING AND YOUR CRYSTALS

You can also program your crystals with intentions. This power charges up your crystal and makes it unique to you and your intention. It is important to set intentions with your crystals.

All crystals have specific properties they naturally hold, but you can enhance and individualise your crystals by setting an intention for the crystal to follow, effectively letting your crystals know specifically what you would like assistance with. Setting intentions with your crystals is a powerful practice that will help you to attract more positivity, healing and abundance into your life. Everything is more potent with an intention, and your crystals are a powerful tool when manifesting and creating Magick.

Crystals have been used throughout millennia for their cosmic healing powers and for their ability to manifest thoughts into reality.

HOW TO SET A CRYSTAL INTENTION!

1. Cleanse

Once you have chosen the crystal or crystals you want to work with to program your intentions, you must cleanse them of any negative energy. You can do this under a full moon, in salt water, using sound healing (singing bowls or tuning fork), or by placing the crystal between both of your hands and sending energy to it to purify and cleanse – visualize sending brilliant white cleansing light to your crystal and spend a minute or two cleansing each crystal.

2. Set the intention

Place your crystal in your hand and take a deep breath, allowing your mind to release any negativity. Speak your intention and command the crystal to now align and action this new intention.

Your intention may be for your crystal to cleanse your mind of chatter or to clear a room of negative energy, or to give you more confidence or similar. Whatever the intention, trust that once you program your intention into your crystal it shall be.

Finish your spoken intention with "so it is" or "so be it".

3. Reinforce your intention

Keep your crystal with you or under your pillow or in the room in which you want to keep cleansed. Each time you look at or touch your crystal remember your intention and say thank you.

Gratitude is a powerful emotion.

Have fun programming your crystals with your intentions.

Not sure what crystal to choose?

The first step in choosing a crystal is to identify what you feel you are missing. This could be love, courage, peace, clarity etc. Or perhaps you want to choose a crystal based on its ability to cleanse or clear energy or protect your space or person.

Identify these areas and then simply allow your intuition to choose for you. If a crystal catches your eye, or you feel a bond or physical pull toward one, know that this is a good sign that this crystal is right for you.

I will cover 12 crystals and their properties and uses. Remember there are far more than 12 crystals available and these are just some of my own favourites. Feel free to research further on crystals and their uses but this will give you a good idea of some popular crystals readily available.

Moonstone

Moonstone cultivates compassion and empathy. It helps you to tap into your intuition and enhances psychic abilities and clairvoyance. Moonstone can soothe feelings of stress and instability so you can move forward successfully. Encourages inner growth and strength.

Amethyst

Amethyst has physical healing properties and is widely believed to heal the mind. A great stone for meditation. Amethyst has the ability to expand the higher mind also enhancing your creativity and passion.

Tiger's Eye

Helps rid the mind and body of fear, anxiety, and self-doubt. A great power and motivation booster. Tiger's eye is also said to help guide you to harmony and balance to help you make clear, conscious decisions.

Citrine

Bring joy, wonder, and enthusiasm to every part of your life with Citrine. Helps to release negative traits like fear, and in turn helps encourage optimism, warmth, motivation, and clarity. Helps with creativity and concentration. Aids digestion and strengthens physical endurance.

Obsidian

A protective stone, Obsidian forms a shield against physical and emotional negativity. Rids emotional blockage and promotes qualities of strength, clarity, and compassion to help find your true sense of self. It may aid in digestion and detoxification, reduces pain and cramps. Blocks psychic attack and absorbs negative energies.

Clear quartz

This white crystal is considered a "master healer." Amplifies energy by absorbing, storing, releasing, and regulating it. Aids concentration and memory. Physically, clear crystals are claimed to help stimulate the immune system and balance out your entire body. This stone is often paired with others like rose quartz to aid and enhance their abilities.

Rose quartz

Rose Quartz is the stone of universal love. Helps to restore trust and harmony in all relationships. Improves close connections and provides comfort and calm during times of grief. Rose quartz encourages self-love, respect, trust, and worth within. Rose Quartz purifies and opens the heart at all levels to promote healing and peace.

Bloodstone

A powerful healing stone, Bloodstone is claimed to help cleanse the blood by drawing off bad environmental energies and improving circulation.

Encourages selflessness, creativity, and idealism and keeps you present in the current moment. Can help to rid feelings of irritability, aggressiveness, and impatience. Heightens the intuition.

Amber

Amber is one of the world's oldest and most coveted treasures. Amber is a natural purifier, esteemed for its ability to draw pain and dis-ease from the physical body, as well as the mind and spirit, by absorbing negative or stagnant energies and transforming them into clear, positive energy. Amber is a stone of protection.

Jade

Jade is a powerful healing stone and used for blessing. Jade can help you access the spiritual world, gain insight into ritualistic knowledge, encourage creativity, and dream-solve.

Selenite

Selenite is an ancient crystal, one of the most powerful for the new vibration on Earth, attuned to the greater good of all beings. It is a beautiful means for accessing and grounding the Light Body. Brings radiance and harmony.

Black Tourmaline

Black Tourmaline is a protection stone, a psychic shield deflecting and dispelling negative energies, entities, or destructive forces. It guards against radiation and environmental pollutants and is highly useful in purifying and neutralizing your negative thoughts and internal conflicts, and turning them into positive, usable energy.

CHOOSE YOU

YOU ARE BEING ASKED TO CHOOSE TO KNOW YOU ARE THE DREAMER OF YOUR DREAMS.

YOU ALONE OWN THEM AND THEY ARE WHAT MAKE YOU UNIQUE.

NURTURE THEM, CHASE THEM, BREATHE LIFE INTO THEM. NO-ONE CAN STOP YOU FROM ACHIEVING YOUR DREAMS.

AFFIRMATION:

I CHOOSE TO NURTURE MY DREAMS.

CHAPTER 9

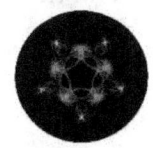

Confused about Manifesting?

Yes, I was confused too. That was until I learned there is no exact formula but there was a way to tap into the free flow of manifestation! Practice, practice, practice. The more you practice, the more you are tuning into your intuition. The more you are connecting with your soul's wisdom. And the more you do this the more you will tap into your inner manifestation Magick.

In truth we are all constantly manifesting. We manifest every experience we have – positive or negative. When I really looked at how to become a Master Manifestor in my life, I realized I was one heck of a fabulous manifestor. It was just that I was manifesting crap experiences. I went through a lot of crap before I realized I was the common denominator. I could manifest relationships, money, and success, but the problem was that I was manifesting the relationships and experiences that would also end up biting me in the butt. The men and relationships I manifested, used and abused me and left me destitute, leaving my reputation in tatters. I will still claim I was very good at manifesting; just not in the right vibration or frequency, therefore the quality of what I was manifesting was low, as were the experiences!

I hope that sparked a bit of a chuckle for you, but in all honesty each of us can manifest. It is how we got here in the first place after all!

The key to becoming masterful at manifesting is simple. It is all about the frequency you vibrate on.

This is the reason I covered the Universal Laws earlier in this book because mastering these laws is the real secret that "The Secret" never told you.

We manifest who we are being. I will repeat that. We manifest who we are being.

Manifestation is not a hustle, nor a struggle. It is a state of being. A state of flow. A simple alignment in frequency. The higher your frequency the more aligned you are in manifesting your desires, not your disasters.

Until you see yourself as a conscious creator, as an attractor, of everything (crappy or not) that comes into your physical experience, you will always feel powerless and will be powerless. You will always pass the blame to an external cause, until you take responsibility. Remember, just as I was the common denominator in my experiences, so too are you in yours.

The first most important step is to take full and total responsibility for everything that happens in your life.

And I mean ABSOLUTELY EVERYTHING. Nothing is by chance and NOTHING IS A COINCIDENCE!

The biggest secret of all is that there is NO FORMULA to manifesting, so stop looking for one. You won't find it.

Manifesting is simply your birthright. You are doing it in every waking moment. It is imperative you begin to align and become a Master of your frequency. That is the secret to becoming a Master Manifestor. If you have been following this guide so far, you will already be letting go of many of the blocks that are standing in your way of being that Woman in Total Control of Herself. This is the inspired action you need to be taking to align your frequency to that of The Universal Laws.

Master your frequency = Master Manifestor.

I have a supercharged activation to help you align your frequency with the Universe by letting go of some of that resistance you have been experiencing. This is the fastest way I know to shift your energy into alignment and become a magnet to the things you truly want to experience.

DIVINE ALIGN ACTIVATE

Before you begin, if you have not already, open your sacred space and ensure you are somewhere you will not be disturbed. As always, feel free to light some candles, play soft, soothing music, hold or place crystals around you, whatever feels right, allow yourself to be guided by your own intuition.

The purpose of setting the scene is to assist you to drop into a space that you will relax enough to allow your higher self to take control. If you find it difficult to relax, invite your spirit to step forward and take charge of your body.

Now take some deep breaths before you start, just centring your energy, and as you exhale let go of any tension, stress or negative thoughts or emotions that are lingering.

Imagine, feel, or perceive a brilliant white light now streaming down through the top of your head (your crown chakra) and this luscious liquid light is now filling your entire body with pure white light. This light is the light of the Great Divine and will assist you in shifting your awareness and raising your frequency. Welcome this loving light into your heart space now.

Say aloud with intention and passion:

"Dear Divine Loving Source,

Please step me into being that Woman In Total Control Of Herself, into my powerful inner WITCH.

I now release all resistance as I surrender fully and let go of all blocks and belief systems, all lower 3rd dimensional energies in the way of me embracing my birthright of abundance.

I send them to you now for transformation. Thank you, thank you, thank you.

I activate my entire energy system to shift my consciousness and to recalibrate into alignment with the Universal Laws to raise my frequency and magically magnetize a life full of blessings, freedom, joy, love, and abundance.

It is my greatest gift to be in my power and I choose this for myself now.

I am a Master Manifestor and I manifest experiences that are in my best and highest good from this time forwards.

And so, it is".

> **WITCH tip:**
>
> Repeat this as often as you feel necessary. Use this activation whenever you feel yourself off your game, or if you have been through a big release of some other negative beliefs or patterns to realign yourself and your frequency. Each time you use it will further align you to Divine Frequency.

Continue to take inspired action, that is action you are intuitively guided to take. Do not worry about how or when your requests will manifest, just know that they will. Keep doing the inner work as this is the key to mastering your frequency and tapping into unlimited abundance, love, joy and happiness.

Journal, dream, and generally feel into your intentions. Do not push, just enjoy. Any action you take should be fun and enjoyable and if it becomes a chore or a struggle let it go. It is meant to feel easy and natural to you. If at any time an action feels forced or fake, or you feel you are making a sacrifice to get it done – stop. Because you are simply trying too hard. Sometimes it looks like nothing is happening, but this is often when everything is happening.

Only take sacred physical action – meaning only take action when necessary or guided by your heart (your Divine Feminine), and until then continue to work on the inner you, this is where the GOLD is at. Understanding how action fits into manifesting will save you a lot of time and bring you into more flow and ease.

Everything you manifest into your life is directly affected by your frequency. When things are going well look at how you were feeling. Begin to bring an awareness and correlation to the times your vibration was high and what showed up for you. Write all your wins, all the miracles, big and small and read over them whenever you need an attitude pick me up.

> **WITCH tip:**
>
> Use the Miracle Book example in the Magic Toolbox to document your wins and miracles.

CHOOSE YOU

YOU ARE BEING ASKED TO CREATE BALANCE IN YOUR LIFE.

MAKE TIME FOR WHAT IS IMPORTANT TO YOU INCLUDING TIME FOR SELF-LOVE AND SELF-CARE,

WELCOME IN NEW ADVENTURES AND EXPERIENCES.

AFFIRMATION:

I CHOOSE TO TAKE TIME OUT FOR ME AND CREATE HARMONY AND BALANCE IN MY LIFE.

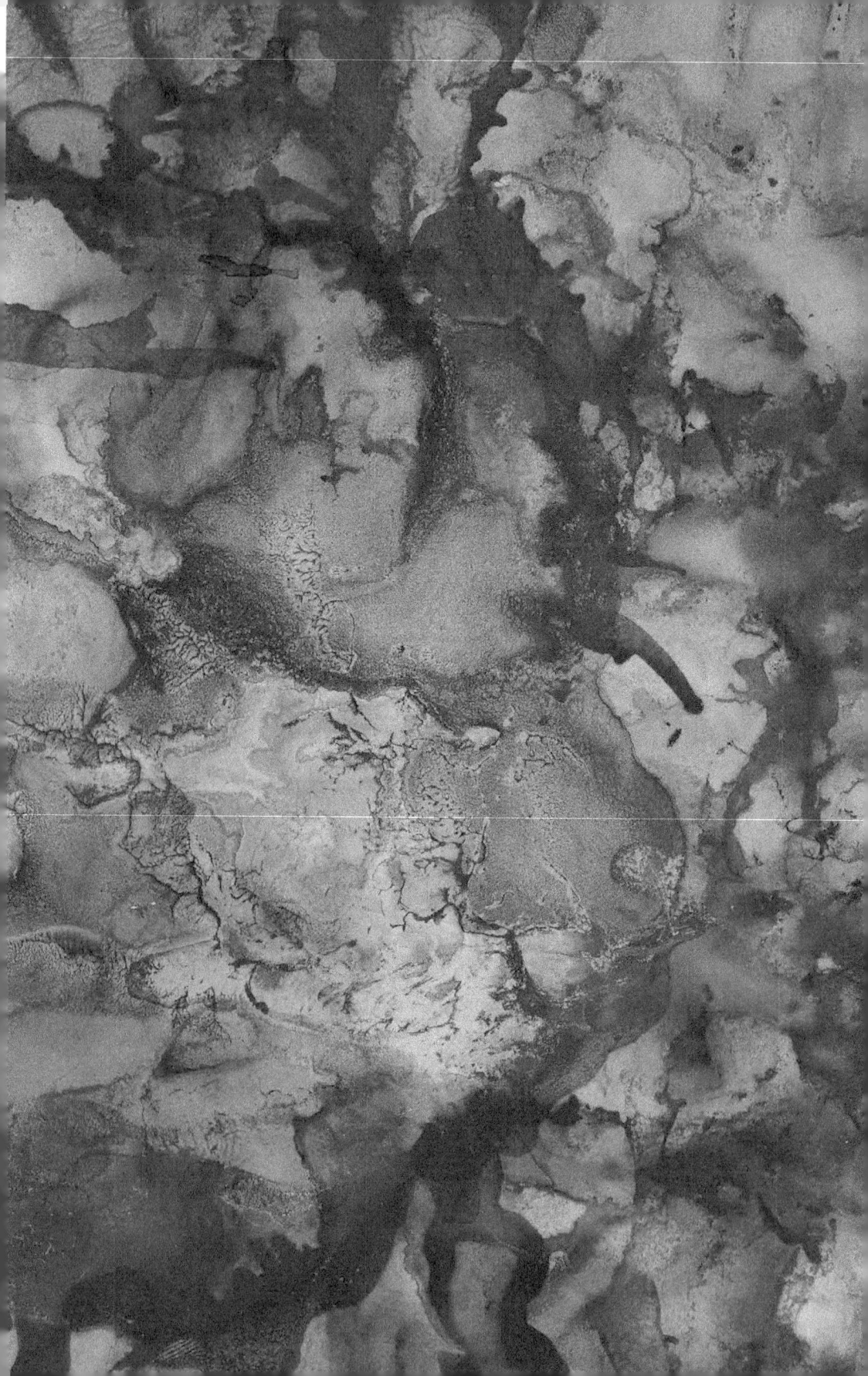

CHAPTER 10

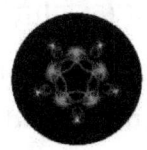

Daily practice. It is all in the cultivation.

Daily practice incorporates the 5 essentials.

1. Dedication
2. Connection
3. Chakra clearing and activation
4. Awareness – mindset
5. Self-love, compassion, and kindness

DEDICATION

Simply put you need to allow yourself some space to truly dedicate to your own rediscovery. Stop the excuses like – "I don't have time" or "I can't concentrate" these are all just a part of that master program (and ego) at play. This is a rediscovery process, not a discovery process. You are rediscovering you.

I find dedication a process of incorporating my entire well-being into my everyday life. I have said it before, that this a lifestyle for me. Not unlike jogging every day or checking social media first thing in the morning, making space for your inner rediscovery is important.

If you do not discipline yourself to cultivate space and guidance for the immense flow moving through you, you are going to be a mess for a very long time. I have provided examples and ways for you to take in daily practice that are enjoyable and will increase your intuition exponentially.

Keep journaling your experience, so you can chart how far you have come. In the Magic Toolbox in Chapter 15, I have included a simple example of a Miracle Book – a mini journal you can write in all your wins, each small and large miracle that you create in your life, jot down in this Miracle Book. When you are feeling down, or feel you have not come far, simply take out your book and begin to read over the everyday miracles that have happened in your life. It is an instant mood shifter and helps you practice more gratitude. There is also an example WITCH journal (you can photocopy if you like) and keep track of how you are feeling. These tools help you to see how far you are progressing.

CONNECTION

Connect into yourself every day and before you know it you will have a continuous connection with your Higher self.

Connecting into Mother Earth daily also is a great way to keep yourself grounded and centred. You could go to the beach, the park, or lie down on the ground for a while, meditating in the beautiful sunshine. Or it could be something as simple as taking off your shoes and standing in the back yard on the grass for 5-10 minutes. It does not need to be difficult, elaborate, or convoluted, you just need to return to your Source energy, and feel the affinity with Mother Earth.

You may also use this Grounding Meditation to assist you to connect and ground your spirit.

> *WITCH* **tip:**
>
> Feel free to record this in your own voice to make it easier to just relax and let go or please feel free to email me at karen@karenstevens.com.au for a download link to this activation from my collection.

GROUNDING VISUALIZATION

Focus on connecting to Mother Earth below.

Get comfortable and know there is no other place you need to be.

Allow yourself to drop into a space where you feel safe, a space where you feel love, if you can, have your feet firmly planted on the floor for this grounding session.

First become aware of your breath. Breathing deeply in and as you do so, breathe in beautiful unconditional love and as you breathe out letting go of all stress and worries.

Breathing in as much as you can and when you exhale feel your body relax.

If you have not already, allow your eyes to close.

Now become aware of the bottoms of your feet as well as the tips of your toes.

Your feet have been taking you so many places over the years and they deserve to fully relax and let go. Place your awareness on your feet and allow them to relax fully. Breathe in deeply feeling comfortable and relaxed. All your attention on the soles of your feet.

Imagine that this is what connects you to Mother Earth. Each step you take has made a difference in your life and moved you through hard times as well as successes and achievements.

Breathe in deeply and send your feet love and respect for everywhere they have taken you in your life. Now imagine the Earth below you, supporting your every move.

The ground is your place of connection and no matter how high up you go or how long your feet are elevated, you always become grounded once again. Become aware of the ground below you wherever it may be and know that it is a source of pure connection to all there is.

Imagine now that from the bottoms of your feet, the roots of your soul are growing and extending down towards the Earth. They connect with the Earth below, and you feel an instant connection and security wash over you, as you are filled with unconditional love.

You feel so totally relaxed as you feel into this amazing connection with the Earth. Feel these roots strong, flexible, and unbreakable. They are now going deep into the Earth and taking root, allowing you to feel totally at peace, safe and secure.

Feeling them grounding you, the soles of your feet are strong and resilient. You have found the link between you and the Earth.

This is a bond that cannot be broken. You came from the Earth and you are always connected to it. Feel the union between you and the soil and feel the Mother Earth and all her love for you.

Allow Mother Earth to introduce you to the power of true connection. You have made a strong alliance with the Earth, grounding you in body and soul.

Now, breathe in deeply again, imagine that you are drawing this powerful experience of connection up your legs, feeling this bond relaxing your body even more as it releases any tension along the way.

Breathe in again, feeling the union of Mother Earth and your body, traveling up into your hips and pelvis.

Breathing fully and passionately, feel the partnership between you and Mother Earth traveling up into your abdomen and ribs. Noticing how being grounded is such a blessing.

Feel the connection travel into your chest and lungs, gracing your heart with love. Mother Earth loves unconditionally, she forever gives and only hopes for care and respect in return.

This deep bond of love is traveling up your neck now, deleting any tension here. This relaxing sensation goes into your entire head, allowing all your muscles and bones to become fully relaxed.

The alliance between you and Mother Earth now travels all the way to the very top of your head.

Notice how you feel right now. You are fully grounded. There is a deep relationship between you and Mother Earth, one that cannot be broken and must always be nurtured.

You and Mother Earth have formed a partnership, one that makes you feel completely loved and cared for. Now hear yourself saying these positive words reflecting true connection to the ground below.

Togetherness
Partnership
Bonded
Unified
Connected
Grounded
Oneness
Love

Imagine again those roots coming from the soles of your feet, they have now grown so deep into the Earth, that you can feel the connection to others around the world. Take some deep breaths and allow yourself to feel this connection for as long as you would like to. There is no hurry.

When you are ready, begin to slowly draw your awareness to the present moment, returning your thoughts to your current surroundings.

Breathe in deeply again, feeling forever connected to Mother Earth and all of her wisdom.

Whenever you are ready open your eyes and give thanks for the Earth and your connection.

Thank you, thank you, thank you.

And so, it is.

Connecting with the Divine and your spiritual evolution team is worthwhile to keep your life force energy connected and clear. You can simply call on their presence when you awaken each morning.

Upon waking I have a lovely practice I partake in. As I open my eyes, I say thank you for the day and that this day will be filled with everything that I love. I say Good Morning to the Divine and ask for assistance from my spiritual team throughout the day with anything that I may require assistance with. I put my hands on my heart and I draw my awareness into this space and say – Heart, lead the way.

This always starts my day off with a surge of love and gratitude and aligns my frequency to a higher vibration.

I have provided a connection activation you can use daily to get you deeply connected to yourself and the Divine, cultivating a deep, unshakeable self-love.

A daily practice of clearing your energy, deeply connecting, and loving yourself unconditionally.

CONNECT ME ABOVE, BELOW AND WITHIN.

Say the following out loud with intention and passion:

"Dear Divine Loving Creator,

Please awaken the awareness within me now that I am worthy of love, abundance, joy, alignment, ease and flow in my life as I now surrender all resistance, all blocks, belief systems, all frequencies less than love from my energy system that are stopping me from embracing my birthright of sovereignty, peace and abundance.

I release them into Mother Earth for transmutation and transformation.

Please assist me to love myself unconditionally now.

With gratitude in my heart I welcome in, receive, and accept your infinite love, wisdom, and guidance.

I open my heart and my hands to willingly receive all the infinite abundance you offer to me.

I follow my heart always, as she knows the way. And following my heart's direction I take inspired action daily to align me to the all loving frequency of my divinity.

And so, it is.

Thank you, thank you, thank you Divine".

CHAKRA CLEARING ACTIVATION

This daily practice will switch on your intuition and clear and activate your chakras, opening your spiritual gifts and switching on your Claires.

This is a part of connecting you to your own Magick and gifts, so I highly recommend you take the 15 minutes every day to do this. If you would prefer the pre-recorded version, you can download it.

Please email me at karen@karenstevens.com.au for a copy.

CHAKRA BALANCE AND ACTIVATION

This clearing and balancing of all your chakras, will bring you closer to yourself and bring a deeper connection with your Divine loving source, clearing the chakras for your chi energy to flow.

Say aloud:

"Dear Divine Loving Source,

Please allow me to release any energies or frequencies less than love now, so I may fully activate and balance my chakras deepening my connection with you and my inner guidance".

Closing your eyes take another deep breath in, allowing yourself to be here. Allow yourself to take in this moment to be who you really are. This moment in time is an important one allowing you to remember who you truly are.

Beyond the external influences in your life, allow yourself to tap into the deep reservoir that is your authentic self.

First become aware of your breath.

Breathing deeply in and as you do breathe in beautiful unconditional love and as you breathe out letting go of all stress and worries. Get comfortable and know there is no other place you need to be.

Allow yourself to drop into a space where you feel safe, a space where you feel love,

Now see white light fill every single cell of your being streaming down into your crown chakra on the top of your head. gently moving through all the way to your toes.

Take another deep breath and as you exhale feel your whole body surrendering and relaxing. Allow any thoughts to simply drift away or place them in a box to deal with later. Allow any sounds you hear to become a part of this meditation.

Give yourself permission to experience this meditation knowing that whatever you experience is in perfect order and harmony with your destiny.

You are now surrounded by your Angels and Spirit Guides.

You hear yourself say "Angels and Guides please surround me now".

You feel safe and peaceful.

Now imagine, see, or perceive that you have a light above your head. This light signifies the essence of the Divine loving source. You feel safe and protected with this light. Allow the light to be any colour that comes to you. It is perfect. If the light changes colour at any time, allow that too. Everything is just as it should be.

Know that you are receiving exactly what you need from the Divine source and your higher self. Trust this process.

You are bathed in this beautiful light. You can feel it on your skin and surrounding your whole body.

Imagine this light now enters the top of your head, your Crown Chakra.

The Crown Chakra is associated with the colour purple.

You allow the light to enter. You can feel any blocks that are blocking the top of your head, melt away with ease. You feel the light opening the top of your head like a flower blossoming. It fills any emptiness you have there.

You hear yourself say, "I now allow the Divine Loving Source to enter me and clarify my thoughts".

You feel a connection to the Source of All. And you feel this light switching on your Claircognisence (this is your knowing).

Pay attention now to the spot between your eyes, your Third Eye. The Third Eye Chakra is associated with the colour indigo or dark blue.

You notice whether your Third Eye is open or closed. The light clears away any blocks inside your head and in front of your Third Eye.

You hear yourself say "I now allow my Spiritual vision to manifest clearly".

You feel your natural Clairvoyance switch on. See your Third Eye open and see this light now entering and filling the area and streaming out of your Third Eye.

The light also clears blocks inside your head where your Ear Chakra is. The Ear Chakra is associated with the colour magenta.

You hear yourself say, "I now allow myself to hear Spirit clearly". Feel your Clairaudience switch on and your Spiritual Ears clear and become receptive.

The light travels down to your throat, clearing a space there so it is easier to breath and speak your truth. The Throat Chakra is associated with the colour light blue.

Feel this light expand your Throat Chakra. Feel any blocks being removed that prevent you from speaking your truth.

You hear yourself say, "I now allow myself to speak my truth with integrity".

The light transforms and expands your Throat Chakra. Notice yourself feeling the courage and wisdom to speak up for yourself and what you believe in.

The light moves down to your heart. The Heart Chakra is associated with the colour green. Notice any blocks and emptiness in different areas in your heart. Feeling the light melting away all blocks and filling any emptiness.

You hear yourself say, "I now allow Divine loving source to fill and open my heart".

Feel your Intuition and Clairsentience switch on. Feel the light expanding your heart Chakra through the front and the back. Feel yourself more connected to all beings. Feeling more compassion.

Feeling safe to allow your heart to open. Knowing this is a gift you give to yourself. Notice this softening and expansive feeling fill your heart. It is safe to love and be loved now.

Feeling this light traveling down now to your solar plexus. The place between your heart and stomach. The Solar Plexus Chakra is associated with the colour yellow. This centre of your being is now filled with this loving light. See any blocks or toxins being dissolved by the light.

You hear yourself say, "I now allow myself to feel powerful". Feeling your self-esteem increase as you feel one with Divine source. Knowing that you indeed are a manifestation of this source. Knowing that you are worthy of embracing the essence of the Divine.

That this is who you are. You are connected to Divine Source in a profound way. You know that as you say yes to the very source from which you are created, so too will you manifest unlimited abundance in your life.

Now the light travels down to your stomach, your Sacral Chakra. The Sacral Chakra is associated with the colour orange. You notice any emptiness replaced and refuelled by Divine loving source. You notice any blocks or toxic waste is being removed.

And You hear yourself say "I now allow myself to feel whole, joyful and complete".

You feel full and peaceful at the same time. The only permanent thing that can fill you here is source energy. All other attachments are temporal and unnecessary. Feel yourself embrace this light with enthusiasm. Feel the joy and certainty of contentment filling your entire body as you accept this Divine source into your stomach.

The light now travels down to your Base Chakra. The Base Chakra is associated with the colour red.

You notice this light fills your base Chakra, the sexual organs and transforms any blocks or emptiness into a completely safe and nurturing feeling.

You hear yourself say, "I now allow myself to completely trust". Feel how it feels to allow Divine Source to be fully housed in your temple.

Feel this light traveling down to your feet. Imagine that your feet have roots at the bottom of them. Feel these roots go down deep into the centre of the Earth. Feel yourself one with the Earth. You are now grounded. Completely grounded whilst being connected to Spirit.

Feel yourself clear and filled with the Spiritual light of Divine loving source through your whole body.

From your Crown Chakra down to your Base Chakra. Feel the light surround you now. You feel the light within your body, throughout the front and back of your body and all around you.

You are filled and surrounded by the Source of All. You are connected above, below, and all around you. Enjoy this feeling and know that this feeling is your birthright.

Feel a celebration now from the Angels and Guides all around you. You are deeply connected; you feel aligned and full of Divine loving energy.

Thank you, thank you, thank you Divine.

As you count to 3 come back into fully waking consciousness remembering this experience and committing to the practice of clearing and connecting daily.

1, 2, 3.

Say aloud:

"I now choose to maintain a continuous and clear connection of energy flowing throughout my energy system. I claim my birthright of connection to the Creator of All that is, to my Divine loving source. It is my gift to be and live in my fullest power.

And so, it is".

4. AWARENESS AND MINDSET

Beginning with a daily practice of mindfulness will establish a good self-awareness and self-knowledge. Mindfulness is the practice of maintaining a moment-by-moment awareness of your thoughts, feelings, body sensations, and surrounding environment, through a gentle, nurturing lens. Mindful meditation can help you connect into this nurturing space. When you practice mindfulness, your thoughts tune into what you are sensing in the present moment rather than rehashing the past or imagining the future.

Self-awareness is the conscious knowledge of your character, feelings, motives, and desires.

How you define yourself at any given moment dramatically affects how you think, feel, and react to everything in your internal and external world. It requires you to dig deeper, embrace constant evolution, and opportunities to learn, it inadvertently leads to a growth mindset.

Self-awareness conditions you to accept and navigate situations with flexibility, which is key to a growth mindset. It also equips you with the knowledge and acceptance of your strengths, and weaknesses, helping you navigate every situation with accountability and self-responsibility.

You need it to build on your mindset. Having a growth mindset (the belief that you are in control of your own ability and can learn and improve) is important as it is essential to developing healthy self-esteem. It is an important tool that affects your daily self-talk and reinforces your most intimate beliefs, attitudes, and feelings about yourself.

Having a good mindset and self-awareness will lead you on the path to emotional mastery. Emotional Mastery is the process of becoming aware of and learning to direct your emotional states – how you feel moment to moment – and using it to your advantage.

All these practices bring you further into alignment as you strengthen the connection with yourself and the world around you.

Try some mindful journaling. Examine what is in your head and in your heart and get it out of your head and onto the paper. Doing this helps you get to know who you really are; your motives, your values, the way you think and the way you feel.

> *WITCH* tip:
>
> Gratitude journaling, doodling, and colouring are all powerful mindfulness exercises too!

5. SELF-LOVE, COMPASSION AND KINDNESS

The act of self-love, compassion and kindness is about nourishing the relationship you have with yourself. Practising self-love, compassion and kindness is as simple as treating yourself like you would your best friend or loved one. You certainly would not speak badly to a loved one or friend, would you? So why would you want to speak harshly or critically to yourself?

Understand that attuning your frequency is all about having love for self, and that even if you are loving, kind and compassionate to others, and neglect to do the same for yourself you are building negative karmic reserves that you will need to balance.

Karma does not play favourites even if you do. When you are not kind or compassionate towards yourself, it Is no different than being unkind or lacking empathy for others. Remember, we are all one. What happens to you, indirectly affects me also and vice versa. This is how the principle of the collective consciousness works. It is the sum average of all thoughts and feelings, so we are all affected in some way by another's thoughts or actions.

Try this self-love/compassion exercise that will help you bring awareness to how you are treating yourself. Are you living in a space of love or judgement?

HOW WOULD YOU TREAT YOUR FRIEND?

Write down your answers to these questions.

1. Think about a time when a close friend came to you for some advice. They were feeling bad about themselves and were struggling. What would you say to your friend? What would be the advice you would give them?

Write down how you would respond to help ease their pain.

2. Now think back to times when you have felt low or were struggling yourself. How do you usually respond to yourself when you experience these feelings?

Write down what you think or say to yourself. What action do you take – if any?

3. Was there a difference between how you would respond to your friend and how you responded to yourself? If yes, why do you think this was?

Write down your thoughts on what makes you treat yourself so differently from others?

4. Write down how things would change if you treated and responded to yourself as you respond to your friends.

Remember to ask yourself – Is this how love would respond?

For the next week practice treating yourself like a good friend and see what happens. Journal around how you felt and what changes you noticed.

A little Magick always goes a long way, so if you are really struggling with being compassionate and kind with yourself, please use the following activation.

SELF-WORTH AND SELF-LOVE ACTIVATION

Before you begin, if you have not already, open your sacred space and ensure you are somewhere you will not be disturbed. As always, feel free to light some candles, play soft, soothing music, hold or place crystals around you, whatever feels right, allow yourself to be guided by your own intuition.

Take a deep breath, get comfortable. Nothing else matters right now but your own personal breakthrough, your own gift to yourself.

Place your hands over your heart chakra and bring all your awareness to your body. Feel your body. Relax into your body. Feel your breath, breathing in unconditional love and feel this love as it spreads throughout your mind and your muscles, from your head to your toes.

Enjoy the feeling of lightness, enjoy the feeling of being calm and relaxed.

Take a deeper breath. Breathing in and out rhythmically.

Drop into the space within, a space where you feel safe, a space where you feel peace, a space where you feel love, allowing the worries of the world around you to fall away, to fall off the left side of your body and off the right side of your body.

Your whole energy is you, vibrating and slowing into a beautiful state of comfort.

Say aloud:

"Dearest Divine Creator of All,

Please allow me to release any frequency less than love now.

I release all feelings and doubts of worth to you now, all negative thoughts and emotions that do not serve my highest good, I release them to you for transmutation and transformation.

I now call upon the blessings of your Divine Grace to activate a deep self-love and compassion throughout my emotional, physical, mental, and spiritual bodies, my DNA, and my subconscious mind, throughout all timelines and frameworks of my existence.

Please restore my DNA to my original Divine Bliss Blueprint so I am reconnected to Unity Consciousness.

Thank you Thank you Thank you Divine. Thank you for blessing me.

And so, it is".

Setting Boundaries

Why is setting boundaries so important?

Setting strong boundaries is an important act of self-love, allowing you to practice self-care and self-respect. Boundaries are essential to healthy relationships and help you communicate your needs and set limits in a way that is healthy and respectful. Boundaries help you to make time and space for positive interactions and aid your entire wellbeing.

Setting and sustaining boundaries is a skill many of us never learned or find it difficult to do and this can lead to resentment and feelings of being used or unappreciated.

Here are some tips to set clear, concise boundaries to protect your energy and practice self-love and respect.

1. Set your limits.

You need to know where you stand before setting boundaries. So, identify your physical, emotional, mental, and spiritual limits. What can you tolerate and accept and what makes you uncomfortable or stressed? Make a list of what you can and cannot accept and this will be your guidelines when setting your boundaries.

2. Know your rights.

You have the right to say no without feeling guilty.
You have the right to be treated with respect.

You have the right to make your needs as important as others.
You have the right to be accepting of your mistakes and failures.
You have the right not to meet others' unreasonable expectations of you.

Once you know your rights and choose to believe in them, it will be easier to honour them. This will stop you using your energy to please others who take advantage of you.

3. Trust your instincts.

If it does not feel right, it is not right for you. Your instincts can help you determine if someone is violating your rights or boundaries or when you may need to set stronger boundaries. Check in with yourself and trust your gut.

4. Values.

What are your values? Make a list of your 5 core values. Reflect on how often those values are challenged. This will let you know if your boundaries are strong or need a bit of tightening.

Signs of healthy boundaries

- Saying no without guilt.
- Asking for what you want or need.
- Taking care of yourself.
- Behaving according to your own values.
- Saying yes because you want to, not because you cannot say no, or

out of obligation or need to please others.
- Taking responsibility for your own happiness.
- Feeling safe to express difficult emotions.
- Not feeling responsible for someone else's happiness.
- Standing in your truth and being unapologetically you!

Another aspect of self-love and boundaries is eradicating toxicity in your life. Removing yourself from negativity and negative experiences and toxic people is one of the greatest acts of self-love.

It can be difficult especially when the source of toxicity in your life is family, so begin by limiting your contact with those that suck the life out of you and drain your energy. Set clear boundaries and stick to them. Be assertive. Learn to say no. Protect your energy and your personal space.

CHOOSE YOU

YOU ARE BEING ASKED TO CHOOSE TO
RELEASE ALL BLOCKS FROM CONNECTING
WITH YOUR SOULMATE.

LET GO OF THE EXPECTATIONS AND ALLOW
YOURSELF TO
FOLLOW YOUR HEART.

I ALLOW MY TRUE ESSENCE TO SHINE AND
ATTRACT DIVINE SOULMATES INTO MY LIFE
NOW.

AFFIRMATION:

I CHOOSE TO FEEL SAFE TO LOVE
AND BE LOVED.

CHAPTER 11

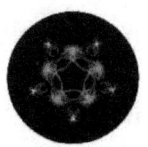

Call in love and your Divine Soulmate connections.

We all want that soulmate connection. That deep, deep connection with our truest Divine soulmate partner. And we also want to have those soulmate connections within our circle of friends, our business, and our lives in general. Connecting with our soul family.

So how do you attract those connections into your life and your awareness?

To begin with, you are on the right track if you have been following along with this guide book. All true relationships and connections start with the self. Self-love and acceptance are a key ingredient to attracting mutually beneficial relationships in every area of your life.

The next step is clearing the space for those relationships to connect and flourish. Releasing all fear around past experiences, healing the old wounding, and forgiving yourself for past mistakes; perceived or real.

This is why this chapter is towards the back of the book, as it is always best to prepare yourself for a true soul connection.

One of the most common things I see with my private clients is that they are blocking the connection to their true soulmates by having unrealistic expectations, judgements and an impatience around timing.

The truth is you have many, many soulmate connections throughout your lifetime. Each soulmate connection, whether it is a soul partner or a soul family member or friend, is intense. These connections help us to grow; to face our deepest fears, release our deepest wounds, and require us to take great leaps of faith and have courage knowing and trusting that everything is as it should be for this moment in time; and that it will be as it should be in every moment of time.

One of the most difficult and devastating things for most people is letting go of a soulmate relationship when it ends. The misconception being that soulmate relationships are destined to last forever, and this is simply not true. Each connection is to further your growth and evolution as a soul. The break-ups can feel as if your heart is being ripped open and you are near death, but this is a part of the process of opening the heart chakra further to allow more love in, more light. The faster you are able to let go and surrender, the faster you grow and the quicker you can shift and align into the energy of your experience, and your next soulmate relationship. Never fear, sometimes your growth may be painful, but it will be so worth it and will lead you closer to the soul connection you yearn for.

Everything that is meant for you in this life, you will experience – no exceptions.

I truly believe that there are no coincidences in life, there are no chance happenings, no luck and no wrong place-wrong time experiences.

EVERYTHING that is meant for you will come to pass, the key to remember here is that you can delay it and hold it up, taking the hardest path possible or you can choose to take the easy-breezy path and surrender into the joy of each and every experience you have. Even the lessons are blessings!

In terms of calling in your soulmate then, how does this apply?

Releasing the old baggage

You will not be able to connect with your soulmate if you are still stuck in resentment or fear. You need to be ready and open to receive the intensity and amount of love that will be coming your way.

If you have issues with trust, betrayal or anger and are still waiting for Karma to get your ex then you still have some hang ups you need to release in order to bring in the energy of a true Divine soul connection. If you still feel stuck go back to earlier chapters in this guide and release the blocks.

Cutting ties with the old and welcoming the new

It is important to clear any old ties or connections with ex-partners if you are wanting to call in your soulmate love relationship. This goes for soul family connections, friends and business partners or clients.

The first step is to choose to disconnect and let go. Keeping an old lover, a business connection or friend just in case or because you fear letting go, will only hinder your efforts to call in the new relationships and experiences you desire. So, you need to make it clear to those connections that you are moving forwards, without them.

The next step is to energetically disconnect from them. This is an important step as there could still be ties and cords binding you energetically to their energy field. You may find that you cannot stop thinking about someone, that out of nowhere the energy and image of someone can flood your mind, thoughts, emotions, and space. Whenever you connect with someone, and they connect with you, this activates an energetic connection between you both – an invisible connection – a cord. These cords can last lifetimes.

Energetic cords can be positive or negative. Cords share and transmit a high frequency of communication between two sources. Positive cords can be a beneficial exchange and you can send and receive loving energies and thoughts, and this can be uplifting.

Negative cords on the other hand are generally created from a space of jealousy, resentment, pain, or fear. They can also create pain, sadness, instability, and fear in your life. They can also stop you from speaking your truth, can cause you to lose or lack confidence and overall can be a physical and emotional drain.

Whilst positive cords are beneficial for our well-being, negative cords need to be removed to help you to separate from lower vibrations and disconnect from unhealthy sources of energy, releasing ties and bonds that are undeserving of your energy matrix and to assist you to start, connect with and be fully present in new positive relationships. Cutting cords with someone can also allow a deeper expression of an existing relationship. By cutting the negative, co-dependent ties that are binding you, it can allow for a new freshness and openness of truth, and new possibilities in your relationships.

It is time to cut those cords!

Use this simple cord cutting method I have perfected to cut ties simply and efficiently – there is no need to repeat this for weeks on end. It works instantly and you will feel differently after using it.

Powerful Energetic Cord Cutting Release

Before you begin, if you have not already, open your sacred space and ensure you are somewhere you will not be disturbed.

You may like to light some candles, play soft, soothing music, burn essential oils, hold or place crystals around you, whatever feels right, allow yourself to be guided by your own intuition and what you connect with.

The purpose of setting the scene is to assist you to drop into a space that you will relax enough to allow your higher self to take control. If you find it difficult to relax, invite your spirit to step forward and take charge of your body and mind. Simply state, "Higher Self step forward and take charge now".

Now take some deep breaths before you start, just centring your energy, and as you exhale let go of any tension, stress or negative thoughts or emotions that are lingering.

Imagine, feel, or perceive a brilliant white light now streaming down through the top of your head (your crown chakra) and this luscious liquid light is now filling your entire body with pure white light.

Say aloud with intention:

"Dearest Divine Loving Source,

I call upon your powers of Divine light, blessings and protection to heal, let go, and cut any etheric cords that are no longer serving my best and highest good.

I request that all cords attaching and binding me and (name of the person you wish to cut ties and cords with) that are not aligned with the frequency of love, light and abundance now be released.

I now sever and release all energetic cords that do not serve my highest good.

I release myself from these binds, contracts, cords and ties and I confirm that all cords and ties are now destroyed across all dimensions, within all space and realities and throughout all frameworks of my existence, never to return again.

I hereby banish these energetic cords and recover now all energy that was harvested or siphoned from my soul or my life force energy.

I confirm the full release of any and all negative after affects or repercussions from this karmic release now.

I send love, light and blessings to myself and (the name of person cords/attachments were with) and seal myself in a protective violet circle filled with brilliant, shimmering, purifying, Divine light.

Take some deep breaths and feel your energy now flowing back to you, filling you once again with vitality and creating a peaceful energetic boundary of love and light.

Thank you thank you thank you Divine.

And so, it is".

WITCH tip:
Essential oils to use for this release are: Sage or Frankincense.
Crystals to use for this release are: Selenite, Black Tourmaline, Smoky Phantom Quartz.

Time to shine. Be the Beacon.

Now you are free of the negative energetic bonds it is time to shine. Literally. It is time to become the beacon to what or who it is you wish to attract.

Make it easier for your soulmate to find you. Shine bright from the inside out. Let your true essence free, share your inner happiness, and radiate love – for others and for yourself.

Take good care of yourself and put aside time every day to do something that will make your heart sing. Remember a soulmate can't make you happy, that needs to come from within.

CALLING IN YOUR SOULMATE

Remember earlier in this chapter, I said that you have many soulmate connections. This is because each connection, each soulmate helps you to grow and evolve by teaching you what you most need to learn at the time, they help to heal those unhealed parts of you as you do for them. They are not here to complete you, because you are not broken, nor are you half of a pair, you are completely whole, and your soulmate is too. Your journey together is one of growth, of deeper connection within you, and to the Universal Law of Oneness. He/she cannot make you happy. Happiness and joy are not dependent on another. It lives within you and this is the role of the soulmate, to help you connect with it through experiencing it within them

I have found with my private clients that the more inner work they have completed the "higher" the quality of connection they experience within their soulmate relationships

I cannot express just how important it is to clear out limiting beliefs and negative patterns, emotions and thought forms.

If you are willing to learn, grow and evolve without having to go down the path of repetitive painful lessons, you can fast track your truest most Divine soulmate connection and enjoy a more evolved relationship that will be a more joyous experience on the whole

I would love to share an exercise I do with my private clients that is both fun and intentional as a preparation prior to the soulmate connection and will have your ideal soulmate materializing into your awareness.

Do this exercise and powerfully call in your ideal man/woman.

YOUR IDEAL MAN

Write down everything you desire about your ideal man.

APPEARANCE

What does he look like?
Hair Colour?
Wavy/straight/curly?
Short or long hair?
Beard or no beard?
Eye Colour?
Height?
Weight?
Muscular/slim/athletic/heavyset?
Dimples?
Scars?
Tattoos?
Piercings?
Does he care about his appearance?

DEMOGRAPHICS

Who is he?
Name:
Age:

WITCH

Location:
Income:
Occupation or life situation:
Business owner?
Hobbies, interests:

PERSONALITY

What sort of person is he?
How would you describe his personality?
What does he like?
What does he dislike?
Is he scientific or creative?
Is he a details person or big picture dreamer?
Dress style? Casual/business/sporty/fashion conscious?

EDUCATION

What does he know?
How educated is he?
Is he still studying?
Has he heard of you before?
Have you known each other before?
If so, how well does he know you?
If you have never met before, how would you want him to get to know you?

PSYCHE

What does he think/believe?

Objectives/goals - what does he want to achieve in life and love?

Opinions/beliefs - what does he think about life in general?

Opinions/beliefs - what does he think about Religion?

Opinions/beliefs - what does he think about Politics?

Opinions/beliefs - what does he think about Sports?

Opinions/beliefs - what does he think about Marriage?

Opinions/beliefs - what does he think about children?

Opinions/beliefs - what does he think about spirituality?

Fears - what are his 3 am fears – what keeps him up at night?

**Feel free to add any other features or desires you have with regards to your ideal partner.

Now you have all the particulars it is time to look up images in Google and place an example of what your ideal partner looks like.

And add to your avatar.

NOW YOU ARE READY TO WRITE HIS STORY.... A day in the life of.... David

David is just an example but if you love him too feel free to use some of his story.

Write the story of your ideal man – this example will help you with the format. Feel free to just let your imagination run wild. Remember you can have anything you desire. If you can dream it, you can create it and "David" will exist. It is a universal law!

WITCH

MEET DAVID

David is a 28-year-old rally car driver. He loves the thrill and excitement of driving fast cars but is safety conscious and aware.

He is single and has dated a couple of girls seriously but has never found that one that really had his heart.

He is 6-foot-tall, dark brown tousled hair and dreamy blue eyes and he has a couple of tattoos tastefully placed on his biceps. He is lean and muscular and enjoys racing – it is his passion.

He is ambitious and focused and has drive and determination. He is looking for a woman who can captivate his heart and is different from the rest.

He is well spoken, concise and has respect for himself and women in general. He has a few mates and they meet up fortnightly for a guy's night of sports watching

He is considerate and kind and has an open mind

He doesn't follow any particular religion and is a bit of a free spirit. He would like to have children in the future and will be a good provider. He has a cheeky side that is well balanced with his empathic nature that alerts him when he is overstepping his mark

He is witty and warm and shows his appreciation and gratitude. He lives in the suburbs and drives a Lexus. He works in corporate and is seeking sponsorship and clothing labels to further his brand – himself; to fulfill his plans to leave the corporate 9-5 and be freer with his time. He is suave and sophisticated and enjoys fine dining and is fun loving enough to enjoy grabbing a bite to eat at the local food stands.

NOW IT IS YOUR TURN TO CREATE.

Or if you prefer -

YOUR IDEAL WOMAN

Write down everything you desire about your ideal woman.

APPEARANCE

What does she look like?
Hair Colour?
Wavy/straight/curly?
Short or long hair?
Eye Colour?
Make-up or Natural?
Height?
Weight?
Muscular/slim/athletic/heavyset?
Dimples?
Scars?
Tattoos?
Piercings?
Does she care about her appearance?

WITCH

DEMOGRAPHICS

Who is she?
Name:
Age:
Location:
Income:
Occupation or life situation:
Business owner?
Hobbies, interests:

PERSONALITY

What sort of person is she?
How would you describe her personality?
What does she like?
What does she dislike?
Is she scientific or creative?
Is she a details person or big picture dreamer?
Dress style? Casual/business/sporty/fashion conscious?

EDUCATION

What does she know?
How educated is she?
Is she still studying?
Has she heard of you before?
Have you known each other before?

If so, how well does she know you?

If you have never met before, how would you want her to get to know you?

PSYCHE

What does she think/believe?

Objectives/goals - what does she want to achieve in life and love?

Opinions/beliefs - what does she think about life in general?

Opinions/beliefs - what does she think about Religion?

Opinions/beliefs - what does she think about Politics?

Opinions/beliefs - what does she think about Sports?

Opinions/beliefs - what does she think about Marriage?

Opinions/beliefs - what does she think about children?

Opinions/beliefs - what does she think about spirituality?

Fears - what ARE her 3 am fears – what keeps her up at night?

**Feel free to add any other features or desires you have with regards to your ideal partner.

Now you have all the particulars it is time to look up images in Google and place an example of what your ideal partner looks like.

And add to your avatar.

NOW YOU ARE READY TO WRITE HER STORY.... A day in the life of Gemma.

*Gemma is just an example but if you love her too feel free to use some of her story.

Write the story of your ideal woman – this example will help you with the format. Feel free to just let your imagination run wild. Remember you can have anything you desire. If you can dream it, you can create it and "Gemma" will exist. It is a universal law!

MEET GEMMA

Gemma is a 30-year-old massage therapist. She loves all things spiritual and enjoys going out to live bands.

She is single and has dated a couple of guys seriously but has never found that one that really had her heart.

She is 5 foot 7 tall, dark brown long hair and dreamy blue eyes and she has a couple of tattoos tastefully placed. She is lean and voluptuous and enjoys helping people. It is her passion.

She is ambitious and focused and has drive and determination. She is looking for a partner who can captivate her heart and is different from the rest.

She is well spoken, concise and has respect for herself and others. She loves catching up with her girlfriends and they meet up fortnightly fa girl's night of movies and fun.

She is considerate and kind and has an open mind.

She doesn't follow any particular religion and is a bit of a free spirit.

She would like to have children in the future and will be a good mother. She has a cheeky side that is well balanced with her empathic nature that alerts her when she is overstepping her mark. She is witty and warm and shows her appreciation and gratitude.

She lives in the suburbs and drives a Jeep. She works in corporate and helps busy workers to de-stress. She is suave and sophisticated and enjoys fine dining and is fun loving enough to enjoy grabbing a bite to eat at the local food stands.

NOW IT IS YOUR TURN TO CREATE.

You can revisit this exercise and the following ceremony anytime you like. Your desires can change, and your ideal partner can get a makeover and upgrade at any time!

Once you have created your ideal partner it is time to send this desire to the Universe.

I like to do this using a tried and tested ceremony. You will need matches, candles or a lighter to burn the paper, and you could include a container that you can burn paper in, either a tin or fire pit are appropriate.

BRINGING YOUR IDEAL PARTNER TO LIFE.

Make a copy of your final draft of your ideal partner.

I like to make two handwritten copies, as hand-writing holds more energy than a computer printer.

Pick a place that holds power or resonance for you. If possible, try to go outside, in nature as having a natural surrounding is more beneficial and is less cluttered with old energy.

I like to be surrounded by trees and the moonlight to witness my ceremony.

Kneel or sit on the ground, and connect with Mother Earth. Take some time to breathe and connect with Her energy.

Place some crystals (Rose Quartz, Moonstone and Selenite are best for your ceremony) in a circle around your handwritten creation. Read your list of ideal traits for your ideal partner as commands, not wishes or prayers.

Do not just read the list, project the emotional feeling of all that you command. Hold the emotion of ALREADY HAVING and KNOWING that your ideal partner is now aware of your energy and is on his/her way to you now.

Once you have finished reading your list and calling in your partner, end your command with a resounding – so it is or so be it!

Then burn the paper (that is why you make two copies). This releases the energy into the Universe, so it can come back to you as you commanded.

Be careful and specific with your wording. Remember, If you name it, you claim it

Keep the other copy of the list and place it under your pillow or in your nightstand or a special place you can lovingly gaze at it occasionally and connect back to the emotion of having this person in your life.

> **WITCH tip:**
>
> This ceremony is more powerful when done under a New Moon's blessings.

Now you have completed the exercise and created your ideal partner, you have released the energy to the Universe and you are ready to connect more deeply, energetically, with your soulmate.

This next step will attract your soulmate into your 3D reality.

The following invocation will assist you to manifest your soulmate by clearing any possible blocks or contracts that may be interfering with your connection.

Soul Mate Attraction Activation

Before you begin, if you have not already, open your sacred space and ensure you are somewhere you will not be disturbed. As always, feel free to light some candles, play soft, soothing music, hold or place crystals around you, whatever feels right, allow yourself to be guided by your own intuition

The purpose of setting the scene is to assist you to drop into a space that you will relax enough to allow your higher self to take control.

If you find it difficult to relax, invite your spirit to step forward and take charge of your body and mind.

Now take some deep breaths before you start, just centring your energy, and as you exhale let go of any tension, stress or negative thoughts or emotions that are lingering.

Imagine, feel, or perceive a brilliant white light now streaming down through the top of your head (your crown chakra) and this luscious liquid light is now filling your entire body with pure white light.

Say aloud with passion and intention:

"Dear Divine Loving Source, the Creator of All that is,

I ask for assistance from all beings of love and higher, the ascended masters, the Lords of Karma, enlightened beings and guardians, my spiritual evolution team, and the full co-operation of my higher self for the soulmate attraction activation.

I hereby banish, release, sever and delete all cords of attachment, all contracts, belief systems and all unresolved karma between myself and all my previous partners for my best and highest good.

I confirm all blocks to my most compatible soulmate in this lifetime have now been removed, cancelled, cleared, deleted, and erased in all directions of time, never to return.

I now step into a new timeline where I now easily and gracefully attract love into my life.

I know and understand that I am worthy of great love and am entitled to all the beauty life has to offer me. Everywhere I look I see love, in every tree, flower, river and all of nature. I feel loved in all my forms now and I open my heart and welcome this love into my heart with joy.

I deeply love and appreciate myself. I am a unique being with amazing talents and I am confident in exactly who I am. I accept myself fully on every level now.

My interactions with others reflect just how deeply I love and accept myself now.

I am regarded as valuable because I value myself. My mind is filled with loving thoughts for myself and others. I am a beautiful, confident, intelligent, powerful, loving and capable woman.

The qualities I desire in my soulmate connections are obvious to me now. I can see them written before me on a big screen within my mind."

- Visualise or perceive this list now forming in front of your eyes, in your mind's eye, on that big screen. Take some time to think of all the qualities you desire.

Say aloud:

"My soul mate is attracted to the values and qualities I possess, and I only attract those connections with those who possess the qualities I seek.

I am now surrounded by connections with others who are ready for a loving soulmate relationship commitment. Those that will give of themselves, spiritually, mentally, emotionally, and physically, freely, and easily.

I request that my energy field be cleansed, strengthened, and upgraded so I now attract unconditional love to myself like a magnet".

-All your energy now floods back to you, filling you with brilliant white light.

See this light now swirl around you in a rapid clockwise spiral and then return to your energy field, giving you a boost of vitality and surrounding you in a sphere of white protective light.

You are now open to love. You know what you want, and your soulmate can see you as clearly as you see them now. You welcome love into your life each day. You have a deep love for yourself and in doing so, you welcome others to love and be loved by you.

Say aloud:

"I, (your name) confirm that all blocks, cords and attachments to previous relationships have now been dissolved with love and gratitude. I am now ready to connect fully with my true Divine soulmate and I choose this for myself now.

And so, it is. Thank you, thank you, thank you Divine".

WITCH tip:

Essential oils to use for this activation are: Rose, Frankincense, Jasmine, White Lotus and Blue Chamomile.
Crystals to use for this activation are: Rose Quartz, Moonstone, Jade and Malachite.

As the days and weeks pass, you will be presented with new opportunities and connections. Keep surrendering into your heart space and continue to fill your heart chakra with unconditional love.

Be the beacon, and your soulmate will see you.

WITCH tip:

You can call in soul friends, family and soul clients using the same Magick – just change your focus from the romantic soulmate connection to the connections you wish to manifest. Intention is everything!

CHOOSE YOU

YOU ARE BEING ASKED TO CHOOSE TO CREATE AND ALLOW MORE SUCCESS, LOVE, WEALTH AND HAPPINESS INTO YOUR LIFE NOW.

LET GO OF THE HOW AND WHEN AND ALIGN TO THE DIVINE NATURE OF ABUNDANCE.

AFFIRMATION:

I CHOOSE TO RECEIVE ABUNDANCE IN EVERY AREA OF MY LIFE NOW.

I AM ABUNDANT.

CHAPTER 12

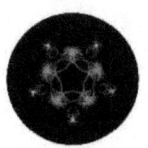

Calling in money, wealth, and abundance.

Do you feel uneasy about having wealth, being rich or having what you want? Or perhaps it is that you feel unworthy, undeserving, guilty or have doubts about ever achieving wealth?

You live in an abundant Universe. Abundance is your natural state of being.

Go for a walk and notice how nature is fully abundant. From the grass that grows in the cracks of the footpath, to the weeds that always seem to need attending to; the flowers that grow out from between seemingly impossible places, to the baby birds squawking in the trees; the sun that shines bright and the rain that falls from the sky.

What we can see in nature is the exact same design that lives within us. The abundance in nature also exists within us. It is our natural birthright. It is who we are, it is how we are designed to be

We have strayed from this knowledge, our beliefs have limited our thinking and it is time to step back into alignment with the frequency of abundance.

Calling in money, wealth and abundance is about the ability to receive, welcome in and accept.

And that ability can be blocked due to mindset, thoughts, patterns, beliefs, curses, and programming.

Each of these blocks affect your energy and your energy is your currency. This is important for you to remember. Far more than any action or strategy you take, your energy will ultimately be the deciding factor to what, how much and the quality of that which you manifest into your life, on every level. Financial wealth is simply a flow-on effect that reflects every other area of your life.

When working with my private clients the first thing I do is identify these blocks so I will share here how you too can identify where your blocks are and how to get to the core of your money woes

The very first thing to do is to identify if there are any old, limiting beliefs around money, wealth, and abundance for you.

Start with this simple exercise to closer examine your beliefs and blocks.

Make a list. Identifying your money beliefs.

Make a list. Write down the list of limiting beliefs you have around money. Some examples may be:

I never have enough!
I always run out!
I can't anyone with money!
Money is the root of all evil!

Money doesn't grow on trees!
I never get paid back when I loan money!
I have to work hard for money!
Rich people are mean and selfish!
Money goes out faster than it comes in!
Money is not spiritual!
Credit card companies are loan sharks!

Think back to your childhood. What were your parent's beliefs around money? Did they discuss their money problems or were their money problems a cause of arguments and unrest? Did they have to work hard for every dollar they had, or were they overly protective of their money? Remember this is not a blame game, this exercise is simply to find out where your core beliefs began so you can clear them. Your parents did the best with what they knew and most likely grew up with the same beliefs they inherited from their parents, as did their parents and so on.

Once you have your list on the limiting beliefs you have around money, I want you to do this exercise again, but this time make a list around your beliefs around money and your self-esteem or identity.

For example, some limiting beliefs around money and self-worth may be:

I do not deserve success!
Everyone else comes first!
I'm not good enough to make money!
I can't afford it!
Artists (healers, spiritual practitioners, musicians etc) have to struggle

hard to earn a living!
I can't charge that much!
I find it hard to value my own potential!
I cannot do what I love because it does not pay well!
I am never lucky!
It is impossible to have it all - a loving family, my dream job, good friends, health and lots of money!
I do not love myself for who I am!
I am always in debt!

Now look over your lists and focus on bringing an awareness and understanding in as to why and where these beliefs formed. Thank your beliefs for how they have protected you and kept you playing safe, but understand now that you are able to move past it and make better choices and form new beliefs in your life

Afterall, you are here in this transformational time on Earth for a reason. You are what is known as the Gatekeeper for your generation. It is time to rise and you are just the woman for the job!

Now go back to Chapter 6 and muscle test around any negative or limiting beliefs or patterns you may have. When you have done that, release them using the reprogramming command. This will take effect immediately and will recalibrate your energy frequency.

Follow up daily by reframing your thoughts. Use the following affirmation activation daily for the next 28 days. You can use this more if you desire but please make sure to do a minimum of 28 days. The affirmation activation is filled with powerful activating Magick that will assist you in accepting the reprogramming and forming new neural pathways to keep the positive change flowing around money and abundance.

MONEY AND ABUNDANCE AFFIRMATION ACTIVATION

Recite daily out loud:

"Dearest Divine Creator,

Please let me release any frequency less than love now. Allow me to let go of all negative thoughts, feelings and beliefs around money and abundance and open my eyes so I may see and know the truth that sets me free.

I release all cell memories stopping me from receiving abundance in my life now

I share the Divine nature. I love and accept all that I am.

My energy is my currency and I am aligned with the frequency of wealth and abundance.

- I am a magnet for money.
- My wealth shines from within me.
- I allow myself to be drenched with financial abundance always, and I generously share my wealth.
- I radiate wealth, abundance, and prosperity.
- My riches are forever increasing as I give more of myself in service to the world.

- My body, mind and soul are beaming with love and abundance.

And so, it is.

Thank you, thank you, thank you".

Now you have identified and released any old, negative, and limiting beliefs and patterns the next step is to clear any past life or generational blocks that could be holding you back from your birthright of manifesting and abundance.

This next invocation will powerfully release and free you from all poverty consciousness, debt systems, materialism and consumerism and all curses and blocks on money and abundance. The purpose of this release is to restore positive wealth openings and blessings of abundance to activate your inherent birthright of abundance in every area of your life, not just your wealth.

POVERTY CONSCIOUSNESS CLEARING AND FULL RESTORATION OF THE ORIGINAL CRYSTALLINE BLUEPRINT

Before you begin, if you have not already, open your sacred space and ensure you are somewhere you will not be disturbed. As always, feel free to light some candles, play soft, soothing music, hold or place crystals around you, whatever feels right, allow yourself to be guided by your own intuition.

"Dear Divine Loving Source, the Creator of All that is,

I request assistance from all enlightened beings of love and higher, the ascended masters, my spiritual evolution team, and the full co-operation of my higher self.

I command the full erasure of:

All poverty consciousness frequencies,
All Egyptian black magic and money curses,
All debt and enslavement programs,
All Power Elite and Cabal control structures,
All addiction, mind control, and materialism programs and false karma,

including all fear-based propaganda and engineering that has been programmed in my DNA, my subconscious mind and archetypal body.

I now download and install my original Divine creation blueprint into my DNA, subconscious mind, and archetypal body of:

Unconditional Love,
Creation,
Abundance,
Joy,
Gratitude,
Freedom, and Oneness.

I now call for full restoration of my 617 living soul facets including full harmonizing of each of the five individual sections therein:

The Word,
The Actus,
The Prima,
The Nomen,

The Spiritual Name.

Activating the words of power,

Arom Nahrea -
Keli,
Lekab,
Lehah,
Sael,
Vaho,
Doni,
Aumem,
Mabeh,
Aiau
- Arom Nahrea.

I now call in, accept, and receive all the blessings of good fortune, prosperity and abundance offered to me from my esteemed spiritual guides, goddesses, angels and deities. Thank you, thank you, thank you. I now request to connect with love coded hydroplasmic light and activate in my human body, the Silicate Matrix DNA template - the original human crystalline blueprint

I am now completely aligned to my original Divine blueprint of abundance.

And so it is".

You have now activated your original Divine blueprint for abundance, not only in wealth and money, but in every area of your life. You are now one will all there is.

The following is an activation to assist you to manifest wealth and abundance into your life consistently. Remember the key to everything is to keep your frequency – your energy – aligned with the Law of Frequency Harmony. Until you master staying in harmony, keep practicing and aligning until you can manage to stay in Frequency alignment often.

WEALTH AND ABUNDANCE ACTIVATION

Before you begin, if you have not already, open your sacred space and ensure you are somewhere you will not be disturbed. As always, feel free to light some candles, play soft, soothing music, hold or place crystals around you, whatever feels right, allow yourself to be guided by your own intuition.

Repeat aloud:

"Dear Divine Loving source please allow me to release all energies and frequencies less than love with ease and grace now. I release all struggle and surrender fully to release all blocks, belief systems and fear in the way of me embracing my birthright of Divine abundance.

I hereby release all the pain, fear and conditioning that has made me feel small and unworthy of financial abundance.

Help me to forgive myself and all others who may have previously made me feel insecure or undeserving of my power and my ability to manifest, receive and accept abundance and money.

I allow my consciousness to shift as I gracefully step into knowing and feeling I deserve love, abundance, wealth, and joy in my life consistently now".

Take a deep breath in then release allowing yourself to get comfortable. Closing your eyes take another deep breath in, allowing yourself to be here. Allow yourself to take in this moment to be who you really are.

This moment in time is an important one allowing you to remember who you truly are beyond the external influences in your life, allow yourself to tap into the deep reservoir that is your authentic self.

First become aware of your breath. Breathing deeply in and as you do, breathing in beautiful unconditional love and as you breathe out letting go of all stress, tension, worry and fear. Get comfortable and know there is no other place you need to be. Allow yourself to drop into a space where you feel safe, a space where you feel love.

Visualise white light filling every single cell of your being streaming down into your crown chakra on the top of your head and gently moving through all the way to your toes. This brilliant white light is clearing and aligning all the chakras throughout your entire body.

Feel this beam of light cleansing and clearing all the stagnant energy that no longer serves you as you feel yourself becoming energetically aligned. Surrender to this warm energy radiating through your whole body. Now quiet your mind and simply relax. Release any resistance.

Repeat aloud:

"Creator of All,

I am ready to be surrounded by experiences that nurture and support me and allow me to fully expand into the truest version of my soul. I trust and I surrender knowing that you are my faithful guide. Please bless me with the same trust and faith in myself

I now choose and align to receiving an abundance of money doing what I love, my passion, as I embrace my energy as my currency

I put myself first now, I take care of my health and in doing so I am able to help those I love

I communicate with strength and clarity and this is expressed in my words and actions now.

My energy is harmonious, consistent, and strong. I am the master of my emotions and my intuition and I am powerful and successful. I have complete trust in myself and the incredible life I am creating filled with love, abundance, flow and ease.

I am sure of myself; secure. I am confident and powerful and any old desperation, fear, lack or need to make my life happen right now is renewed with a sense of calmness and peace.

Every cell of my body sparkles with the energy of love, clarity, and power.

I honour and trust myself.

Even though I do not definitively know the path to the future, I honour and trust the path I am taking will lead me to my best future. A future of love, abundance, and success in my life.

I take inspired action; I follow my intuition, and this fills my heart and soul with such joy. I listen to my soul, connect with my heart and this moves me into a deep trust and flow and as I focus intently on my heart's desires this powerfully magnetizes abundance into my life.

I welcome in, receive, and graciously accept a continual flow of money consistently with ease and flow now, as I shift from fear into love, the financial miracles continue to flow in. I gracefully and gratefully accept this as my normal now.

I declare, I no longer sacrifice my desires, dreams, wishes, or needs. I am a powerful manifestor and the master creator of my life. I am abundant and aligned with the frequency of abundance. I continuously and consistently create abundance with ease, grace and flow.

I am a money magnet.
Money flows into my life easily and is attracted to my energy.
I am a miracle and I attract miracles in my life consistently.
I am aligned with the energy of money.
My energy is my currency."

Place your hands over your heart and your solar plexus chakras and imagine, sense, or perceive sending loving energy to these areas. You are opening your heart and activating your soul's wealth energy prosperity.

You are a wealthy, loving, talented and powerful woman. And you love the woman you are and the woman you are becoming.

Thank you, thank you, thank you for rising up and thriving.

And so, it is"

> **WITCH tip**
>
> Essential oils to use for this activation are: Frankincense, Jasmine, Orange, Patchouli. Crystals to use for this activation are: Pyrite, Citrine, Jade, Clear Quartz, Amazonite.

Now you have energetically cleared and restored your positive wealth energy centres, it is important to keep your energy and frequency aligned.

Practice journaling around your wealth desires, performing an abundance ritual (see below) and continue to embody the feeling and thoughts of abundance. Have an attitude of gratitude and know you are blessed with Divine Abundance as your birthright

If any negative thoughts, emotions, or fears arise be swift in reframing using the affirmation activation.

ABUNDANCE RITUAL

This is a powerful and potent simple ritual for manifesting abundance and prosperity into your life.

These cheques can usher in abundance in unseen ways into your world and can unfold in many ways. Be grateful for the prosperity and abundance already in your life and keep yourself open to the unfolding.

THE UNIVERSE
THE BANK OF UNIVERSAL ABUNDANCE

DATE: _____

PAY TO _____

THE ORDER OF_____

$

_____DOLLARS

BANK OF UNIVERSAL INTENTIONS TRUST
1111 Magical Place
Prosperity City, The Universe

SIGNATURE_____

THANK YOU   THANK YOU   THANK YOU

Photocopy one of the abundance and prosperity cheques above. Place your name in the "Pay to" section. On the next line write "paid in full" where you would usually write a dollar amount. If you wish to ask for a certain amount, you can place it in here.

Sign the cheque with "The Law of Abundance". You can choose to leave the date blank or you can put a date on it if you wish to see when the abundance will come to you.

Add affirmations to your cheque writing ritual to create even more attraction to abundance:

"I am open to abundance"
"I am deserving of prosperity"
"I am open to the ways that abundance manifests into my life"

"I am thankful for the blessings and prosperity on their way into my life"

"I am thankful for the abundance in my life and welcome more"

"I am an abundant, courageous, Magickal, manifesting queen"

> **WITCH tip:**
> Use crystals that attract abundance and prosperity: Citrine, Green Aventurine, Tiger's Eye, Jade, or Sunstone are powerful prosperity crystals.

Light a candle dedicated to prosperity and abundance or choose a candle that resonates to you.

You can even anoint it with an abundance oil: Ginger, Frankincense, Myrrh, Patchouli and Bergamot are powerful prosperity drawing oils that can be used to anoint your candle.

You can call upon the Goddess of Abundance Lakshmi, or the Lord Ganesha of Abundance and Wealth to be present with you and work your prosperity ritual.

Place your cheque in a safe and sacred place. A dedicated abundance box or in a night table with your gratitude journal would be perfect.

Release control of how and when the abundance will flow to you. Be open and let the Universe take care of the details

Be sure to be present with gratitude for the abundance in your life presently and offer deep thanks as your cheque is being released. Be Open and allow.

> **WITCH tip**
>
> My energy is my currency.
>
> Keep your energy and frequency aligned – everything that shows up in your life is a direct reflection of the harmony of your frequency. Check in with your vibes regularly and continue to use the Magickal tools provided.

CHOOSE YOU

YOU ARE BEING ASKED TO CHOOSE TO LET GO OF THE PAINFUL MEMORIES STORED IN YOUR CELLULAR MEMORY AND DNA.

LET GO OF THE CELL MEMORIES THAT ARE AFFECTING YOUR BODY, MIND AND SOUL.

RELEASE THE TRAUMA AND TRANSFORM IT WITH LOVE.

AFFIRMATION:

I CHOOSE TO HEAL MY BODY.

I LOVE AND HONOUR MYSELF.

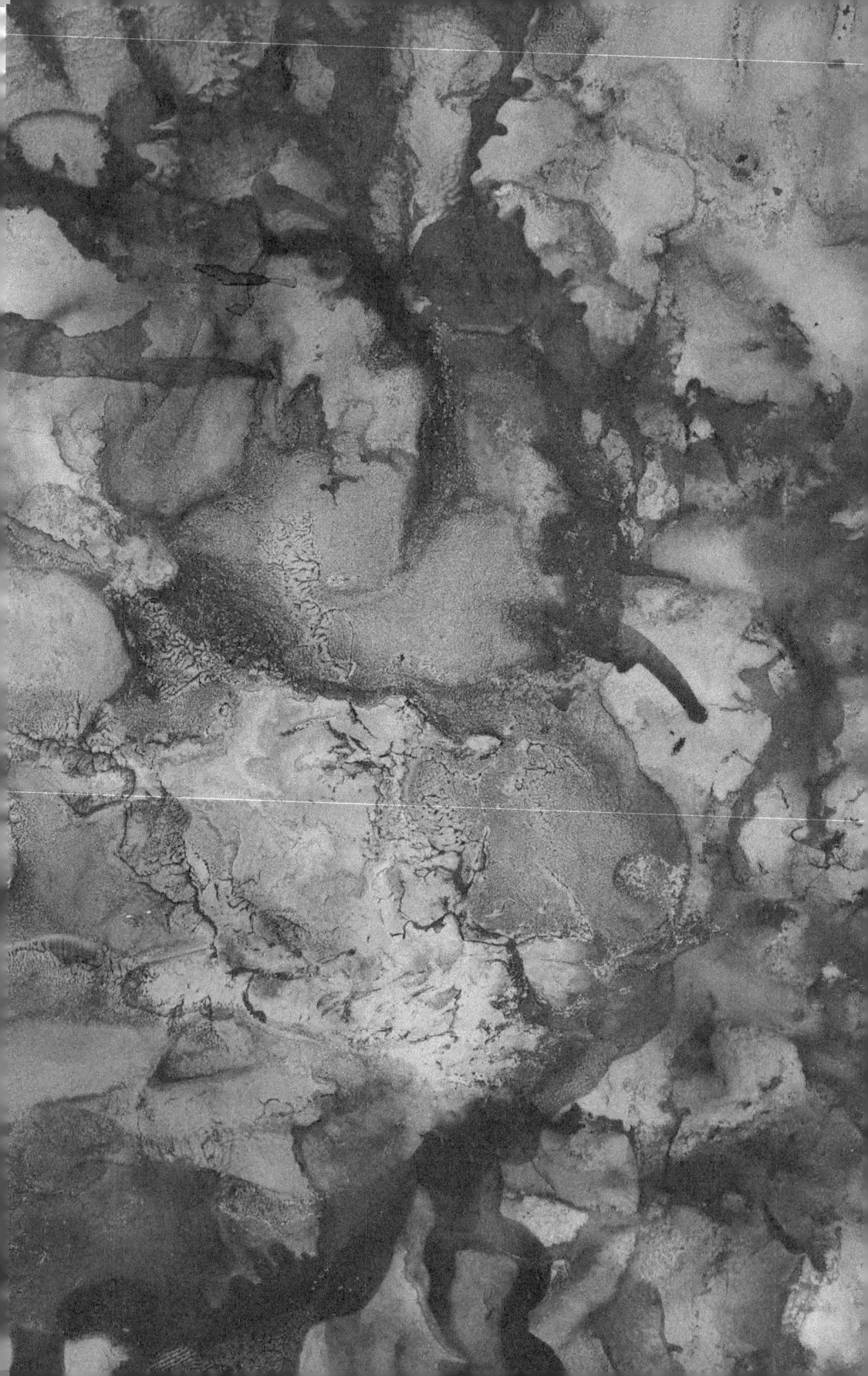

CHAPTER 13

Improving your health.

Your health is so much more than your physical wellness, your health is the wellness of your entire energy system.

For me, this was one of the most profound moments in my own healing journey, when I became aware of how I could heal my health in its entirety.

I had suffered immensely in my life with chronic diseases and pain and was always put in the "too hard basket" by the medical profession and sent away without a clear diagnosis or any real treatment plan that was effective. It was always about numbing the pain or keeping the pain stabilized, and not even top specialists could not diagnose me sufficiently or effectively. I was treated with heavy drugs like Arava and Methotrexate, Endone and Codeine, Insulins, Anti-coagulants, Blood pressure medications and more. Not one of those medications ever brought me any relief. I was trapped in a world of pain and could see no way through.

I had had hundreds of tests costing thousands of dollars – and none of which got me any closer to better health, reason, or diagnosis.

I am not criticizing the medical profession as I believe they have much to offer in treating acute symptoms, emergencies and required surgical procedures, but I am also highly aware that there is so much they are yet to understand when it comes to our bodies, our minds and our overall well-being.

It was not until I let go of the idea that the medical profession would ever find a treatment for me that would work, was I able to find a way to heal myself.

I tried many holistic therapies and although I would find some relief for a short period of time, the pain would always return. The problem was that the treatments were not focusing on my entire energy system. I found they were also focusing on the symptom not the root cause just as the medical profession did.

The more I learned about energy the more I found a connection within myself. This connection ultimately is what guided me into developing my own integrated techniques and style to release the pain and the cause of that pain. You see the pain was just the messenger, getting louder and louder as each year passed, and the more I squashed down my feelings, thoughts, and dreams, the more inauthentic I became, and the more pain I would suffer.

This was the epiphany I had been searching for.

I could probably write an entire book focused on healing pain and will most likely do so in the future; I am sure, but please know, if you follow this guide from start to finish you will experience significant release from your pain as you work through each step. This is because pain is just the messenger and as you release old past hurts, beliefs, and negative thoughts, you will undoubtedly be releasing the messages (the pain).

Pain is connected to emotion. When under stress for example you may find you get a headache or tightness in the neck, shoulders, back or jaw. As the emotion compounds so does the pain and it causes an inflammatory response in the body.

Trauma on the other hand, including one-time, multiple, or long-lasting repetitive events, affects everyone differently. Some individuals may clearly display criteria associated with Post Traumatic Stress Disorder (PTSD) or CPTSD - Complex Post Traumatic Stress Disorder or other mental health issues. The impact of trauma can be subtle, insidious, or outright destructive.

Traumas can be considered anything that keep you locked in a physical, emotional, behavioural, or mental habit. The energy of the trauma is stored in your body's tissues (primarily muscles and fascia) until it can be released. This stored trauma typically leads to pain and progressively erodes your health. The importance of clearing trauma and stress from the body is evident for health and wellness on every level - physical, mental, emotional, and spiritual.

If you suffer from chronic pain, or pain that comes and goes, these tools and releases will work alongside every other chapter in this book and will assist you to achieve better health – physically, emotionally and spiritually.

I truly believe everything has a spiritual solution. Everything can be manipulated for a positive result, just as it can be manipulated for a negative result. Everything is energy and energy can transform. Therefore, your health can transform too.

Let us look at each level of our health separately and work through balancing and harmonizing the energy, physical, emotional, and spiritual bodies.

First, we will look at the body as a whole energy system. Your body is an entire energy field full of light, vibration, and frequency. Each of the energy centres (the chakras) all have a corresponding colour. There are 7 major chakras, 21 minor chakras, 86 micro chakras in the human body. Of these 114 chakras, 112 reside within the body and 2 are outside the body

The energy body also contains 72 thousand Nadis.

Nadis are the pathways that your life force energy travels throughout the body. Nadis and Chakras alike are not constructed of a physical matter and cannot be seen in physical form but without them your body could not function, your heart would not beat and your lungs would not move; yet these subtle energy channels give you your very breath of life. I will cover the 7 main chakras here as these are the major purification and distribution centres of energy in the body and assist us with maintaining a consistent flow of life force energy throughout our entire body.

Below is a description of the chakras together with a guide to how you may feel if your chakras are unbalanced and what to expect when the chakras are balanced and in flow. I have included some information about which Crystals you can use to assist with balancing and further information regarding which Archangels can help with activating each chakra.

THE ENERGY BODY

The seven major chakras

Crown Chakra

Situated outside of the body just above the head. The Crown Chakra helps you to connect to your Claircognisence. Connects you to Spirit to refuel with Spiritual energy.

Symptoms when blocked – depression, learning difficulties, weak faith, anger at Divine, brain fog.
Feeling when balanced – strong faith, universal love, intelligent, aware, wise, understanding.
Experience when overactive – dogmatic, judgemental, spiritual addiction, ungrounded.

Associated with the colours white and purple. Crystals such as Clear Quartz and Amethyst can be used to energize and balance this Chakra.

Assisting Archangels:

Archangel Uriel will bring you messages through your Claircognisence.

Archangel Metatron will help you to focus and process this information clearly.

Third Eye Chakra

Situated between the brows. The Third Eye chakra assists you with Spiritual vision and Clairvoyance.

Symptoms when blocked – poor judgement, lacks focus, poor imagination, cannot see beyond the physical.

Feeling when balanced – imaginative, intuitive, clear thoughts and visions, sees beyond physical

Experience when overactive – nightmares, delusions, hallucinations, obsessive, see too many spirits.

Associated with the colours dark blue and indigo. Crystals such as Sodalite or Lapis Lazuli can be used to energize and balance this Chakra.

Assisting Archangels:

Archangel Jeremiel will help you to clearly see the truth in your life.

Archangel Raziel will help you to transform what you see into creating what you want.

Throat Chakra

Situated in the throat area. The Throat Chakra assists you to speak your truth and to speak up for yourself with integrity.

Symptoms when blocked – cannot express self or speak out, misunderstood, secretive, not a good listener.

Feeling when balanced – Confident expression, clear communicator, creative, diplomatic.

Experience when overactive – opinionated, loud, critical, gossip, yell or talk over others, harsh words.

Associated with the colours light blue. Crystals such as Turquoise and Aquamarine can be used to energize and balance this Chakra.

Assisting Archangel:

Archangel Michael holds the sword of truth and works to help you with this Chakra.

Heart Chakra

Situated in the middle of the chest area. The Heart Chakra assists you to feel open and connected to your heart so that you feel compassion for yourself and others. This is the heart of your Intuition and Clairsentience. The Heart Chakra brings a feeling of oneness between you and others.

Symptoms when blocked – lack of empathy, bitter, hateful, trust issues, intolerant.
Feeling when balanced – peaceful, loving, compassionate, tolerant, warm, open.
Experience when overactive – jealous, co-dependent, self-sacrificing, give too much.

Associated with the colours pink or green. Crystals such as Aventurine, Emerald and Chrysocolla help to energize and balance this Chakra. Rose

Quartz crystal, which is pink, is known as the heart crystal. Use this here as well.

Assisting Archangel:

Archangel Raphael works strongly with the Heart Chakra energy in healing.

Solar Plexus Chakra

Situated in the upper belly at the diaphragm. The Solar Plexus Chakra is your ultimate power centre. We feel the essence of the source here. The Solar Plexus is associated with your self-esteem, personal power, abundance, fear of lack, unworthiness, not being good enough, self-worth issues and any shame relating to who we are.

Symptoms when blocked – low self-esteem, feeling powerless, inferiority complex, unable to speak up for yourself or to speak your truth. *Feeling when balanced* – confident, feel in control, personal power, drive, good self-image,

Experience when overactive – over emotional, fixated on sex, hedonistic, manipulative.

Associated with the colour yellow, like that of the sun. Crystals such as Yellow Calcite, Tiger's Eye, Golden Topaz, and Citrine help energize and balance this Chakra.

Assisting Archangels:

Archangel Ariel, the abundance Angel and Archangel Jophiel for embracing your inner and outer beauty, are wonderful assistants for this Chakra.

Sacral Chakra

This is your Joy centre. When you are resourced here you will have a feeling peace and purpose. You are connected to your sensuality and your creativity. You will feel full. Your attachment issues appear here when you feel empty and want to fill yourself up with other things e.g. food, money, sex, alcohol, people, work etc. When you feel empty you will sometimes try to get things to replace pure joy. That is why we need more and more of them to feel good. Pure joy is limitless and that is why replacements of this joy turn into addictions.

Symptoms when blocked – low libido, fear of intimacy, no creativity, isolated.
Feeling when balanced – passion, creative, healthy libido, optimistic, open.
Experience when overactive – over emotional, fixated on sex, hedonistic, manipulative.

Associated with the colour orange. Crystals such as Orange Calcite, Carnelian, Amber, and Citrine will help to energize and balance this Chakra.

Assisting Archangels:

Archangel Gabriel is a great helper here to aid us in feeling nourished and full so that we have the energy to do our creative projects.

Archangel Raphael also fills those areas of emptiness with healing energy to aid in addiction recovery.

Root Chakra

This Chakra involves your trust, safety, and security issues. Your aim is to resource this area so that you feel grounded and that your survival needs are being met. When you are grounded with spiritual support you will feel safe, resolve trauma, and move out of your fight or flight responses. When you are not grounded, your will is disabled; you are not in your body, can behave immoderately and your decisions will not be from your Higher Self. So being grounded and feeling safe on this Earth is absolutely of paramount importance. When unbalanced or blocked this Chakra is the number one reason behind physical, mental, emotional illnesses and addictions.

Symptoms when blocked – fearful, anxious, financial instability, ungrounded.
Feeling when balanced – safe, secure, centred, grounded, happy to be alive.
Experience when overactive – greedy, lust for power, aggressive, materialistic, cynical.

Associated with the colours red, black, and brown. Crystals such as Red Jasper, Garnet, Ruby, Black Obsidian, Smoky Quartz, Black Tourmaline will help to energize and balance this Chakra.

Assisting Archangels:

Archangel Michael helps to ground us and Spiritualise our will, so that we can take Spiritualised action in this life.

Archangel Metatron helps us to focus our will towards creating what we want whilst being in line with the highest good of all. It is the Spiritual entry and exit point.

Balancing the Chakra

Clearing and balancing the Chakras is important to maintain a continuous flow of life force energy throughout your body.

A daily practice of clearing and connecting is important to maintain good connection. Use the Chakra Clearing and Activation in Chapter 10 (or find this in the Magic toolbox in Chapter 15).

Sometimes we need a little extra support as one or more of the Chakras becomes blocked. The following activation will clear the blockages, release the negative energy, and align and attune your entire Chakra and Nadial system.

ALIGN, UPGRADE AND BALANCE THE ENERGY SYSTEM

Before you begin, if you have not already, open your sacred space and ensure you are somewhere you will not be disturbed. As always, feel free to light some candles, play soft, soothing music, hold or place crystals around you, whatever feels right, allow yourself to be guided by your own intuition.

Take a few moments to connect in with your higher consciousness. Take some deep breaths and relax.

Say aloud:

"Dearest Divine,

I request access to the powerful Universal Blue Star Light frequencies to balance, realign and activate my entire Chakra and Nadial system to reconnect, align and attune my physical and spiritual bodies. I release any negative or obsolete subtle energies, and any frequency less than love now.

I request full upgrade of my Nadial structure, my angelic human 12 Strand DNA silicate matrix and my original Diamond Sun blueprint".

Bring your focus in now to your breath and visualize or perceive a beautiful sphere of Blue Star Light now connecting with your breath, moving throughout your body and filling you with this healing light with every breath you take.

Breathing into the heart space, bring your awareness here now.

Continue to breathe deeper while focused on the centre of your heart.

Take a deeper breath in and on the exhale intend to push your breath downward, pushing your breath down the centre of your body and into your pelvis, and pushing your exhaling breath further down and outward for a complete release.

Repeat this exhaling downward breath pattern three times.

Say aloud:

"With gratitude I accept the full reconnection and activation of my energy body.

Thank you, thank you, thank you

And so, it is".

THE PHYSICAL BODY

Your physical body is the vessel that your spirituality, emotions, and creativity flow through. The physical, emotional, mental, and spiritual bodies are vibrational fields of energy that overlap and affect one another. Your physical body can inform you of your surroundings, if something is wrong or right, if there is danger, and if there is pleasure. The physical body can also be affected by your thoughts, your emotions, the foods you consume and things like chemicals and toxins. The physical sensory organ of the skin allows you to feel sensation, to feel pleasure and pain and is your first point of contact with the 3D world you live in.

The physical body is intended to be used to feel and experience a situation. The key to the physical body is to learn to interpret, to feel the messages the heart sends out through the physical body; learning to feel and respond to the messages is how to find balance and harmony. When you become disconnected from your heart, you become disconnected from your physical body, and therefore pain and disease manifest, as you are no longer communicating or feeling the messages from the heart. As the heart continues to send the messages, they become trapped in the physical body and cause inflammation as they build up, never truly being felt, or understood.

It is important for you to work through this guide, chapter by chapter, to reconnect to your heart, to release old patterns, beliefs, and negative thoughts as each of these elements affect the physical body.

I use the following command to realign my physical body and release all trapped trauma from my DNA. This is used in conjunction with each section as a fast and efficient way of releasing any lingering energies trapped in the physical body.

Physical Upgrade

Before you begin, if you have not already, open your sacred space and ensure you are somewhere you will not be disturbed. As always, feel free to light some candles, play soft, soothing music, hold or place crystals around you, whatever feels right, allow yourself to be guided by your own intuition.

Take a few deep breaths and connect into your higher self, your power centre and the Divine.

Say aloud

"Dear Creator of All that is,

Please assist me to release all toxins including all vaccine toxins, physical and emotional traumas, disease, allergies, dehydration, inflammation, and any and all nutritional deficiencies from my physical body.

I now choose to release all physical pain associated with past life deaths or torture, and all cell memories affecting my body. I release all causes of my physical misalignment, through all timelines, throughout all space and realities and all frameworks of my existence.

I request my physical body be reconnected, aligned, attuned, and all my DNA now be upgraded and recalibrated to my original Divine blueprint. I choose sovereignty from this moment forwards.

Thank you, thank you, thank you.

And so it is".

WITCH tip:

Harmonize the body and nourish with foods known as rainbow foods. These foods hold the highest vibration for your body and are natural foods the colours of the rainbow.

Fruits such as strawberries, apples, mangoes, watermelon, blueberries, pineapples, kiwi are an example. And vegetables such as pumpkin, carrots, spinach, squash, corn, red cabbage, eggplant just to name a few. You get the idea. Foods the colours of the light spectrum of the rainbow harmonize our bodies as we too consist of light waves.

THE EMOTIONAL BODY

The word emotion itself means "energy in motion". Where your thoughts and feelings go the energy flows. Your emotional body holds all your emotional experiences, pleasant and unpleasant. Painful, traumatic, or hurtful experiences that you have encountered throughout your life are stored as layers of memory within your subconscious and unconscious minds, and these are the drivers behind your daily thoughts and feelings. If you have not looked at or healed your inner wounding, these past wounds hold you into a negative energetic pattern and influence your everyday life. Every time you feel out of control emotionally or are triggered by a situation, this is a reaction to this inner wounding that needs healing.

The emotional body also houses love (our positive emotion). Anytime you feel something is good or pleasant, the heart is communicating through this positive emotion and you feel joyous, you feel the love, and this is the ultimate state of being.

Healing the layers of emotional wounding allows you to experience this love and joy more often instead of just in momentary glimpses throughout your life. This is each of our life's purpose; the fulfillment of the heart and the honouring of all that is joyful, harmonious and unconditionally loving. Again as with each level of the body, follow this guide to clear and heal the wounded parts of self, and reconnect you to your birthright of unconditional love.

Use this chart to release emotions from your body that are sitting at the surface and are ready to be released. This will give you a sense of relief, calmness, and peace. This is a simple exercise you can do daily to aid your emotional health and wellbeing.

EMOTIONAL RELEASE CHART

1. Fear	2. Guilt	3. Shame	4. Anger
5. Resentment	6. Unappreciated	7. Sacrificed	8. Hurt
9. Unworthy	10. Depressed	11. Grief	12. Abandoned
13. Jealous	14. Inadequate	15. Foolish	16. Desperate
17. Anxious	18. Weepy	19. Nervous	20. Resistance

Using your new skill of muscle testing, test how many emotions you need to release. For example, test between 1-10 or more if needed. When you know how many emotions you must release, then test which of the 20 emotions in the chart it is you need to release. You can break this down into smaller chunks by testing between 1-10 and 10-20 and so on.

Once you have your list of emotions, use the following command to release them.

Say aloud:

"Dearest Divine

I call upon your Divine grace and blessings to assist me to release the following emotions.

(List emotions)

With love, blessings and gratitude for the lessons, wisdom and understanding these experiences and emotions have served.

I now choose to clear and transmute these emotions into spiritual compost and send them back to Mother Earth to be alchemized into unconditional love.

Thank you, thank you, thank you.

And so, it is".

Take a few deep breaths and release all the residue down through your base chakra and into Mother Earth.

THE SPIRITUAL BODY

When the physical, mental, and emotional bodies reach a state of harmony and balance, the higher vibration of your spiritual body is activated. This begins the ever evolving and unfolding of your spirit, your life purpose, your mission that opens the doorway into enlightenment and higher states of consciousness. Use the spiritual body activation to connect your 12 layers of the tree of life.

ACTIVATING THE SPIRITUAL BODY – TREE OF LIFE ACTIVATION

Before you begin, if you have not already, open your sacred space and ensure you are somewhere you will not be disturbed. As always, feel free to light some candles, play soft, soothing music, hold or place crystals around you, whatever feels right, allow yourself to be guided by your own intuition.

Say aloud:

"I call for the assistance of The Creator of All, my spiritual evolution team, and my higher self to activate and awaken my full spiritual body.

I command the full removal of the false matrix and all global control systems to enable the activation and reconnection of the 44 DNA codes containing the records of all that I am.

I request activation of the double-helix, two strands of physical DNA, determining the characteristics of my physical body and the 10 strands of etheric DNA containing the entire history of my soul, my spiritual essence, and the truth of who I really am.

Activating the words of power:

Arom Nahrea -
Keli,
Lekab,
Lehah,
Sael,
Vaho,
Doni,

Aumem,

Mabeh,

Aiau

- Arom Nahrea.

I now access Pure Divine Universal Source energy to activate the 12 layers of my DNA,

Layer 1: The Tree of Life - the courage to move ahead and integrate my fears.

Layer 2: The Blueprint of Life – the ability to focus on something and follow it to completion.

Layer 3: The Present Consciousness Awakening - maintaining gender balance between male and female power.

Layer 4: The Belief Layer - balance between my energy field and physical body.

Layer 5: The Awakening Self– the ability to live peacefully in a state of acceptance.

Layer 6: The I Am That I Am Layer (this is the most sacred and Divine layer) – the strength to stand in my truth regardless of the outcome.

Layer 7: The Balance Layer– the ability to accept both my dark and light sides.

Layer 8: The Truth Layer – the ability to hold personal boundaries regardless of outcomes.

Layer 9: Opening the Blind Eye (or Seeing without Illusion) – the ability to accept and live within a diverse community.

Layer 10: Remembrance – the ability to tune into and listen to my soul, my higher-self.

Layer 11: Realization – the power to envision, create and manifest my visions in 3D.

Layer 12: God (or the Creator) – the ability to be accepting, kind, and appreciate the value in all things.

I now align my energy with the Cosmic Trinity and confirm my sovereignty to the benevolent universal and galactic matrix.

Thank you, thank you, thank you.

And so, it is".

You are now powerfully anchored into the benevolent and organic universal matrix. Your soul aligned to the attributes of your true Divine nature, and your Divine spark, the inner flame ignited.

CHOOSE YOU

YOU ARE BEING ASKED TO CHOOSE TO
BE COURAGEOUS.

KNOW THAT IT IS THROUGH FEAR THAT YOU
GROW AND LEARN MOST.

EMBRACE THESE OPPORTUNITIES WITH
DETERMENATION AND COMPASSION.

AFFIRMATION:

I CHOOSE TO BE COURAGEOUS.

I AM A LEADER.

CHAPTER 14

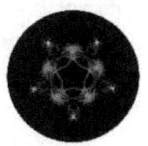

Want to delve deeper into the W.I.T.C.H Shift and how you can help other women activate their Magick?

So, this all sounds amazing, right?! You would love to help other women activate their Magick!!

Well you can, and at the same time you will be helping yourself.

CERTIFICATION COURSE

The W.I.T.C.H Academy will be offering a W.I.T.C.H certification course designed specifically to awaken your gifts and intuition, to teach you the modern day spell work I use with my private clients who achieve amazing, permanent results. It is a cumulation of 20+ years of research, practice, and methods I have tried and tested to ensure they are the fastest, most potent, permanent results of anything that is available in one standalone course.

Not only will you have a certification that will allow you to work with and assist other women, you can build a business or further upskill your current business or coaching practice. You will expand your own awakening into a Woman In Total Control of Herself, becoming a leader and guide for others to follow and aspire to.

The Great Awakening has begun, and you will play an important role in assisting other women to awaken their innate gifts and talents and assist the planet to evolve and prosper.

The certification course will be extensive, with tools for you to increase your own intuition, a program, spell book and oracle cards that are easy to follow, complete detailed explanations that will leave you with no doubt and a greater wisdom and understanding of the ways of the wise woman.

The WITCH that is within us all.

WITCH SHIFT ONLINE PROGRAM

The WITCH SHIFT online program is currently being created and will be available soon for those that want to dive deeper into the connection with themselves in a self-paced online format, with group support and including all tools and materials required.

Please email for upcoming release dates or with expressions of interest to

karen@karenstevens.com.au

DEEP TRANSFORMATION - WORK ONE ON ONE WITH ME PERSONALLY

Deep transformation. This is where the transcendental Magick happens.

I have assisted women to heal from all forms of abuse. I have worked with women to overcome lifelong anorexia, years of trauma and abuse, healing deep-seated family and relationship trauma, chronic diseases, low self-worth, anxiety, depression, and addictions.

The transformation is fast, safe and life changing.

If you are interested in working with me 1:1 personally please email expressions of interest to karen@karenstevens.com.au.

I have limited spaces available and current waitlists are in effect.

TESTIMONIALS

"Thank you Thank you Thank you. You have been an absolute god send to me and my life!!! I Truly am so very grateful for you! The best part of the experience with you was that my life changed dramatically. I am a confident happy woman with so much motivation and determination and I love myself!!!! On a scale of 1 - 10 I honestly have to say 1 million % and more. You are amazing in what you do and how much love, patience, and empathy you put into it helping change the lives of women like me. I absolutely admire you! I know I will continue to grow because of working with you. Thank you thank you thank you!!!" Kristi – NSW

"From the moment Karen Stevens' photograph jumped out of the YMag at me I knew that was a sign! I was curious so I emailed right away. Karen responded within a day and before I knew it, we were having our phone meeting to see whether we would be a match. Sure enough, Karen was definitely able to help me with getting my professional and personal life to the place I could only dream of. I've always had an awareness that I have a special gift to share with others, I just wasn't sure how to go about it and felt my life to this point was in repeat of so much trauma and heartache. Now that Karen has used her gifts, depth of knowledge and expertise, my whole life has shifted to a place I have been longing for. When your life keeps throwing you traumas even when you are feeling good and positive and have good energy, it was still not enough. It was as though everything was trying to hold me back and not live my true authentic life. I know the journey that I'm doing now could never have come through in this lifetime if I hadn't had Karen to help me break through everything that's been holding me back.

I have now truly begun a new lifetime in this lifetime. I feel freed and light and spacious for the first time in 45 years. A deep Joy and Love that I now have each and every day. I now have the confidence, self-love, trust, belief, and empowerment to move forward in my life in every area. So many relationships in my family changed for the better almost instantly and some in the following days and weeks after my sessions with Karen. It is almost too hard to describe and put into words what an incredible, life changing, uplifting exciting experience to have with Karen.

I will forever be grateful for meeting Karen and all that she has done for myself and my family. It is truly priceless to have had this experience. I would highly recommend Karen to anyone wishing to live the best life imaginable and to bring that into your life today. Karen is a true blessing to this world." Mykala - QLD

See more on my website – www.karenstevens.com.au

CHOOSE YOU

YOU ARE BEING ASKED TO CHOOSE TO
STEP INTO YOUR INNER WITCH.

PRACTICE DAILY. PRACTICE OFTEN.

CHOOSE TO BELIEVE IN THE WOMAN
YOU ARE BECOMING.

OPEN YOUR HEART AND ALLOW THE LOVE
AFFAIR WITH YOURSELF TO BLOSSOM AND
WITNESS YOUR CONFIDENCE SOARING.

AFFIRMATION:

I CHOOSE TO BELIVE IN ME.

I AM A WOMAN IN TOTAL
CONTROL OF HERSELF.

CHAPTER 15

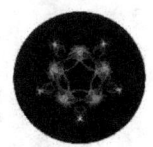

Your magic toolbox.
Use this toolbox jam packed with all the invocations and extra bonuses.

This toolbox is filled with all the invocations and activations in the one space. Use it as a reference guide to keep all your Magick in the one place. There are added bonuses and clearances for your home and your aura and journal examples for you to copy and note take.

If there are any of these activations you would like to have as a recording please email me at karen@karenstevens.com.au to get access to the library of pre-recorded activations and meditations.

Witch Journal

Here is a space to journal your thoughts and feelings, bearing witness to them. Allow your emotions to flow releasing them to paper to transform them.

How am I Feeling?

_____
_____
_____
_____
_____
_____
_____
_____
_____
_____
_____

Everyday Miracles

A space to write your wins and magickal moments. Your everyday miracles big and small.

miracles, magick & moments

miracles, magick & moments

MUSCLE TESTING

Bring your awareness into your hands. Form two intertwined circles with thumb and index fingers

Start with your writing hand (or dominant hand) and place your thumb to your index finger. Then loop your other hand's thumb and index finger through the first "circuit". This creates the electrical circuit you will test the response with

Firstly, you will begin by asking, "What is a YES answer for me"? Quickly pull your dominant hand away from the nondominant hand. Notice whether the fingers stay locked or unlock after you have asked the question.

Do this again by asking, "What is a NO answer for me"? Again, quickly pull your dominant hand away from the nondominant hand, noticing whether the fingers stay locked or unlock after you have asked the question. Be sure that the amount of pressure holding the circuit fingers together is equal to the amount of your testing fingers pressing against them. Use an equal and continuous pressure.

While learning, start by using practice questions. For example:

My name is (insert your name)
My name is (insert someone else's name)

I live in (insert your suburb or country)
I live in (insert a different suburb or country)

So, whilst holding your fingers "in circuit" ask the question … muscle test.

Please note - this is not a competition of strength! Just keep a light connection. You want to be relaxed and in flow when you ask the question.

Example Diagram

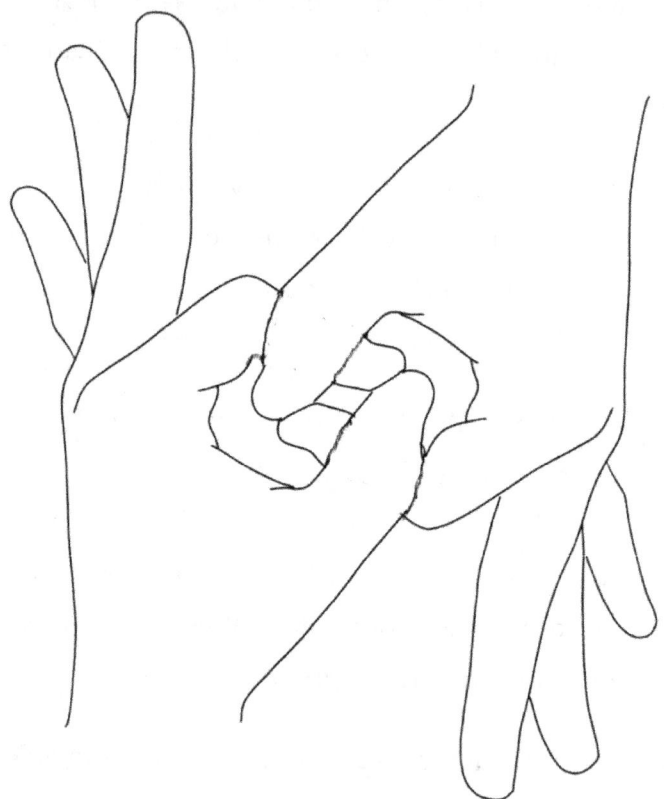

Once you have mastered this and feel confident in your Yes/No responses move on to questioning anything and everything.

OPENING SACRED SPACE

I (your name) now allow myself to be a pure, clear conduit and connection to all that exists. I call upon the assistance of Divine Source Energy and the Divine power of the Golden Ratio including the 5 elements of the Pentagram – Earth, Air, Fire, Water and Spirit. I unlock the words of power – Arom Nahrea, Keli, Lekab, Sael, Vaho, Doni, Aumen, Mabeh, Aiau, Arom Nahrea and I seal my intentions with love and blessings.

Thank you, thank you, thank you.

CLOSING SACRED SPACE

I request cleansing and closure of all gateways of access to all other dimensions and realities

I release all thought forms, beings or energies that are no longer of service to my highest good, across all planes of my existence, across all Universes, all lifetimes and all dimensions of time and space.

I give thanks to all those who assisted me, and I ask that all energies less than love now be transmuted for the highest good of all.

And so, it is.

AURA CLEANSE

A simple and effective aura cleanse to release any negative energies in or around your auric field.

Rub a few drops of essential oil (choose any oil that you love) between your hands to activate it.

Relax and take a few deep breaths.

Imagine purifying golden liquid light now pouring down over you as it streams from just above your head, your crown chakra.

The golden liquid light is encasing your entire body, smoothing down any tears or rips in your aura as it cleanses, purifies, and releases all negative energy from your auric field.

Now run your hands from your head all the way down to your feet as you wipe down your aura.

Say aloud:

"I clear all negative energies from my aura, and I seal myself in white purifying light.

And so, it is".

HOUSE CLEANSE

Say aloud:

"I call upon the powers of the Divine, to powerfully release and dissolve all negative energies, imprints and attachments, spirits, and lost souls from my home and surrounding areas".

Visualize brilliant white cleansing light now filling your home, entering every space, and filling every crevice and gap with this light. This light is purifying and dissolving all the negativity, all the darkness, and releasing the negative imprints from these energies.

Now see yourself being sealed in white and gold protective light, and see this protective light expand out all around you creating a shield of protection all around you, your home, and your family.

You are now protected with Divine Light.

And so, it is.

WITCH tip:

You can use sage to smudge, or burn essential oils of Lavender, Lemongrass or Frankincense.

RESTORE BLESSINGS FOR PROTECTION

Take a couple of deep breaths, imagine now beautiful, pure, golden light is filling your heart space, filling you with more light, more love, more peace, and more freedom. This light now streams out from your heart and expands outwards and all around you creating a seal completely around you, connecting and strengthening the Etheric, Astral, Mental and Causal layers of your auric field.

Say aloud with intention:

"I now call upon Divine Protection and Divine Blessings to keep me safe and protected.

I accept the blessings of Divine Grace and the restoration of my DNA to my original Divine Bliss Blueprint.

I am ready to leave the past and move forwards in leaps and bounds, into my fullest expression and soul essence.

I accept all that Universe Source has to offer me for freedom, abundance, peace and love and I call in these miracles and blessings now.

Ana Bekoah

We beg thee with the strength and greatness of thy right arm,

Accept your people's song, elevate, and purify them,

Please, powerful one, those who pursue your uniqueness,

Guard them as the pupil of an eye,

Bless them, purify them, have mercy on them,

May your righteousness always reward them,

Powerful and Holy One, in goodness lead your people,

Unique and almighty one, to your people turn,

Who remember your Holiness,

Accept their cries, and hear their pleas,

Oh, knower of mysteries,

Blessed is the name of his noble kingdom forever and ever.

Thank you, thank you, thank you.

And so, it is".

DIVINE ALIGN ACTIVATE

Now take some deep breaths before you start, just centring your energy, and as you exhale let go of any tension, stress or negative thoughts or emotions that are lingering.

Imagine, feel, or perceive a brilliant white light now streaming down through the top of your head (your crown chakra) and this luscious liquid light is now filling your entire body with pure white light. This light is the light of the Great Divine and will assist you in shifting your awareness and raising your frequency. Welcome this loving light into your heart space now

Say aloud with intention and passion:

"Dear Divine Loving Source,

Please step me into being that Woman In Total Control Of Herself, into my powerful inner WITCH

I now release all resistance as I surrender fully and let go of all blocks and belief systems, all lower 3rd dimensional energies in the way of me embracing my birthright of abundance.

I send them to you now for transformation. Thank you, thank you, thank you.

I activate my entire energy system to shift my consciousness and to recalibrate into alignment with the Universal Laws to raise my frequency and magically magnetize a life full of blessings, freedom, joy, love and abundance.

It is my greatest gift to be in my power and I choose this for myself now. I am a Master Manifestor and I manifest experiences that are in my best and highest good from this time forwards.

And so, it is".

SPIRITUAL MIRRORS PROTECTION – PERSONAL PROTECTION

See yourself inside a bright purple pentagram, the sides are like laser light beams of all beautiful shades of purple; indigo, lavender, violet, magenta, and lilac.

Powerful white light is cleansing you from every direction.

Repeat aloud:

"Dear Creator of All, please protect me with Divine Protection and surround me with your powerful protecting light.

I now seal this light completely around me, strengthening my aura".

A column of dazzling, shimmering, vibrant Divine Light is now coming down through your crown chakra, filling your entire body, cleansing, and healing every part, every cell, and every organ of your body. This Divine Light now spreads an arm's length all around you in every direction creating a shield of Divine Light that protects you.

This shield of Divine Light is covered with reflective spiritual mirrors, and is spreading Divine Light all around, continuously protecting and shielding you and your loved ones with brilliant, white, liquid Light. Repeat aloud:

"All my chakras are now cleansed, healed, and balanced and I am connected to my full spiritual protections at all times. My channels of communication with the Divine Loving Source are clear and concise, activated fully and I am protected with Divine Protection.

My higher self, always acting in my best and highest good, is now fully in the driver's seat, and my guides and my protection angels are all now working alongside me, assisting me with all that I require for my soul's evolution, freedom and sovereignty.

Thank you, thank you, thank you.

And so, it is".

EVOKE THE ASSISTANCE OF AN ARCHANGEL

The following invocation will connect you to the Archangel you would like guidance and assistance from. Use it to call upon the angels for support and to feel protection when you may be feeling vulnerable.

Say aloud:

"I request the assistance of Archangel (insert your angel's name) to help me with all I require at this time, and to shower me with their healing grace and powers, with blessings and love, magic and miracles. And that Archangel (insert your angel's name) will guide, protect and bring awareness to all the things that I require for my soul's advancement so I am blessed with experiences that are in my best and highest good. Please wrap your wings around me and offer me a safe place to fall and assist me in connecting with my infinite wisdom.

In gratitude I thank you Archangel (insert your angel's name) for accepting my request.

Thank you, thank you, thank you for bestowing your grace upon me.

And so, it is".

CONNECT TO YOUR SPIRITUAL EVOLUTION TEAM

Say aloud:

"I now invite my full spiritual evolution team including all guides, angels and ascended masters to connect with, offer assistance, guidance and healing to me as I may require. I give my full permission for my team to work closely with me to guide me back into alignment with the love of the Universe, to protect me and bring awareness to all the things that I need for my soul's advancement. I am hereby opening the channels of communication with my spiritual evolution team and with a grateful heart I acknowledge this connection and declare it so".

Call on your team anytime. You do not need to have a problem to talk to them. They are there to hear you out, offer assistance, comfort and support.

DAILY GUIDANCE MEDITATION

Close your eyes and take deep breaths. Breathing in through the nose and exhaling through the mouth. Keep focused on your breath and feel it moving through your body, in and out.

Feel your muscles relaxing. See a beautiful golden white light streaming down from above as it now enters the top of your head (your crown chakra). You can now see the light moving through your body and as it does you feel your whole body surrendering and relaxing.

Allow any mind chatter to now just drift away or place it in a lock box to deal with later. Allow any sounds you hear to become a part of your meditation. Give yourself permission to experience this meditation knowing that whatever you experience is in perfect order and harmony with your destiny.

Imagine now that you are walking along a shimmering golden pathway. You feel at peace and are relaxed. As you walk along, up ahead you see a door at the end of the path. It is a lime green colour and it feels inviting. This lime green door is the door to your heart and your soul and as you walk up to the door, you place your hand on the door handle. You feel a tingle of excitement as you open the door and walk through.

Stepping through the door, the most magical space appears. This is your sanctuary. A place you can visit anytime you like. It feels safe here. Protected.

Notice where this safe space exists in your body.

The sanctuary is filled with the most beautiful garden and trees and there is a beautiful body of water in the centre of this space. It is inviting as you walk over you look at your reflection in the body of water. The water sparkles and as you look at your reflection you see that this is a reflection into your soul. An opportunity to connect deeply with your higher self and receive guidance, love, and support.

Start by asking for guidance and by being open to the insights you receive. Set the intention to connect with your spirit and let your inner voice speak to you. You can ask for clarity, your next step, which path is best and for help in making decisions.

Just allow any information to flow through into your awareness now.

Everything is as it should be. Spend as long as you like here deeply connected with yourself and your higher guidance.

When you are ready simply say thank you to your soul for sharing and look once more at your reflection and say – I love you (your name) and I will visit again soon.

As you walk away from the body of water, you take in the beauty that surrounds you. You walk back towards the lime green door and again place your hand on the door handle as you bid farewell to your sanctuary and promise to return soon. As you step through the door and back onto the golden pathway you feel the warmth of the sun on your cheeks, the wind in your hair and you feel your body returning to the present moment.

You wiggle your toes and open your eyes and you are now back in the room with full memory and awareness of your experience.

Once you have finished the meditation come back to your journal and allow your higher self to speak to you and come through your writing. You will have full memory of your connection with your higher self.

GROUNDING VISUALIZATION

Focus on connecting to Mother Earth below.

Get comfortable and know there is no other place you need to be.

Allow yourself to drop into a space where you feel safe, a space where you feel love, if you can, have your feet firmly planted on the floor for this grounding session.

First become aware of your breath. Breathing deeply in and as you do so, breathe in beautiful unconditional love and as you breathe out letting go of all stress and worries.

Breathing in as much as you can and when you exhale feel your body relax.

If you have not already, allow your eyes to close.

Now become aware of the bottoms of your feet as well as the tips of your toes.

Your feet have been taking you so many places over the years and they deserve to fully relax and let go. Place your awareness on your feet and allow them to relax fully. Breathe in deeply feeling comfortable and relaxed. All your attention on the soles of your feet.

Imagine that this is what connects you to Mother Earth. Each step you take has made a difference in your life and moved you through hard times as well as successes and achievements.

Breathe in deeply and send your feet love and respect for everywhere they have taken you in your life. Now imagine the Earth below you, supporting your every move.

The ground is your place of connection and no matter how high up you go or how long your feet are elevated, you always become grounded once again. Become aware of the ground below you wherever it may be and know that it is a source of pure connection to all there is.

Imagine now that from the bottoms of your feet, the roots of your soul are growing and extending down towards the Earth. They connect with the Earth below, and you feel an instant connection and security wash over you, as you are filled with unconditional love.

You feel so totally relaxed as you feel into this amazing connection with the Earth. Feel these roots strong, flexible, and unbreakable. They are now going deep into the Earth and taking root, allowing you to feel totally at peace, safe and secure.

Feeling them grounding you, the soles of your feet are strong and resilient. You have found the link between you and the Earth.

This is a bond that cannot be broken. You came from the Earth and you are always connected to it. Feel the union between you and the soil and feel the Mother Earth and all her love for you.

Allow Mother Earth to introduce you to the power of true connection. You have made a strong alliance with the Earth, grounding you in body and soul.

Now, breathe in deeply again, imagine that you are drawing this powerful experience of connection up your legs, feeling this bond relaxing your body even more as it releases any tension along the way.

Breathe in again, feeling the union of Mother Earth and your body, traveling up into your hips and pelvis.

Breathing fully and passionately, feel the partnership between you and Mother Earth traveling up into your abdomen and ribs. Noticing how being grounded is such a blessing.

Feel the connection travel into your chest and lungs, gracing your heart with love. Mother Earth loves unconditionally, she forever gives and only hopes for care and respect in return.

This deep bond of love is traveling up your neck now, deleting any tension here. This relaxing sensation goes into your entire head, allowing all your muscles and bones to become fully relaxed.

The alliance between you and Mother Earth now travels all the way to the very top of your head.

Notice how you feel right now. You are fully grounded. There is a deep relationship between you and Mother Earth, one that cannot be broken and must always be nurtured.

You and Mother Earth have formed a partnership, one that makes you feel completely loved and cared for. Now hear yourself saying these positive words reflecting true connection to the ground below.

Togetherness
Partnership
Bonded
Unified
Connected
Grounded
Oneness
Love

Imagine again those roots coming from the soles of your feet, they have now grown so deep into the Earth, that you can feel the connection to others around the world. Take some deep breaths and allow yourself to feel this connection for as long as you would like to. There is no hurry.

When you are ready, begin to slowly draw your awareness to the present moment, returning your thoughts to your current surroundings.

Breathe in deeply again, feeling forever connected to Mother Earth and all of her wisdom.

Whenever you are ready open your eyes and give thanks for the Earth and your connection.

Thank you, thank you, thank you.

And so, it is.

IMMERSION - FILLING MY TEMPLE WITH LOVE

Focus on your breathing. In and out. Breathing in unconditional love and as you breathe out simply releasing all tension, fear, stress or worry. Deeply breathing allow yourself to relax completely.

Repeat aloud:

"Dearest Divine Loving Source of All that is, please now release all emotions that are not love with ease and grace. "

Place your hands over your heart space and bring your awareness into this space now.

See the light turn on in your heart and as it does the light becomes brighter and brighter as it expands further and further outwards from your heart space.

In this light you feel safe and you can now see that you are surrounded by angels, guides, enlightened beings, guardians, and your ascended masters, and they are all sending you their love, guidance, protection, and support.

They are here to heal you and fill you completely with Divine Love and Oneness.

This light expands and you realize that this light is your consciousness. This is where you can connect anytime.

It is a place where you are safe, a place where you feel peace, and a place where you feel love.

The light of your consciousness continues to expand past the heart and forms a huge bubble of light all around you.

Expanding your consciousness allows all of your problems and worries to simply fall away – to fall off the left side of your body and the right side of your body.

They simply vanish as you expand your perspective and fill with more love and light.

Enjoy floating in this light and expanding your consciousness and your awareness.

As you float in this light, this calmness, you feel the freedom and the peace of being connected to the Universe and to all of Mother Earth.

In the brilliant glow of the light, you can see all the people who have ever supported you, now walking towards you. They are all right there now in your presence, in your consciousness.

You look at their faces and you can feel their love healing you, you can feel it filling your heart and expanding it with pure joy and unconditional love.

Experience the power of what love can do and the power of healing that it has.

As you feel into this love, I want you to now think about all the love that you have given to those you love. And now send this enormous wave of love to your own heart and fill your heart with this incredible love so you can feel the very same love for yourself.

This is who you really are, this is who you are here to be, and this is what you are meant to experience.

Pure, unconditional love.

Now choose to be this love, to feel this love and to embrace this love. For you are so loved.
You are love.
You are cherished.
You are adored.
And you are precious.
You are fully supported by the Universe in Divine Love and Oneness.

Repeat aloud:

"Thank you, thank you, thank you, Divine.

And so, it is".

UNCONDITIONAL LOVE ACTIVATION

Closing your eyes, getting really relaxed and comfortable now, taking a deep breath in and as you breathe out just allow any tension to leave your body.

A channel of gold shimmering pure white light is now entering the top of your head through the crown chakra) and is streaming down into every cell of your body.

You are relaxed, safe, and calm.

Please read this out loud:

"Dear Divine Loving source,

Please let me release any frequency less than love now.

Allow me to let go of all negative thoughts, feelings and beliefs that are not in my highest good.

I request full removal of all blocks, programs and implants restricting my connection.

I now allow myself to release all conditions I placed upon myself and my worth.

I release myself from these conditions fully.

Please connect me into unconditional love and activate the frequency of 528hz.

Pure, unfettered, boundless and whole.

True love, forever and unchanging.

All four loves - affection, friendship, romance, and unconditional love.

Unconditional love is pure and selfless. Divine loving oneness."

Feel yourself relax, melt, let go and surrender into this state of oneness. Into pure unconditional love.

See this love now filling your heart.

Allow your heart chakra to open fully, breaking open to reveal your true self.

In all your pain, fear, doubts and worries, and in all your beauty, strength and truth, as the angels now come in to assist and take away the stresses, allowing only the nourishment of unconditional love to completely fill the heart space now and connect you deeply into your true essence.

Unconditional love now travels throughout each and every cell, bringing a tingling, bubbly, sparkling energy throughout your entire body.

You are content, fulfilled, nurtured, and feel incredible love coursing through your veins, pumping from your heart and spreading all around your body to the very tips of your fingers and toes.

Place your hands over your heart now and pull your awareness back into this space as your heart whispers messages of positivity, joy, and deep, deep love to you now.

You are loved.
You are adored.
You are cherished.
You are precious.
You are safe.
You are supported, always.
You are a Divine creation and you are beaming with love.

Please read the following out loud:

"I (your name) confirm my heart chakra is now cleared, cleansed and activated and is now vibrating to the 528hz frequency of pure unconditional love.

I choose to stay connected to this vibration, to live in my power consistently, from this moment forwards.

And so, it is.

Thank you, thank you, thank you Divine".

CLEANSE AND UPGRADE YOUR DNA BLOODLINES AND ANCESTRAL LINES AND ACTIVATE YOUR W.I.T.C.H DNA.

Please read this out loud with intention:

"In the Name of Christ Consciousness, in the name of our Sacred Earth that registered the footsteps of my lineage, I request the blessings of Divine Light and Manifestations of Eternal Love from every vibration of the Cosmic Mind, to travel down now to the roots of my genealogic tree, as a balm of forgiveness and absolution.

May this blessing be bestowed upon my ancestors, releasing, curing, and healing old wounds, old patterns, and compulsive behaviours. Transmuting, purifying, and alchemizing all generational curses, all persecution energy stored in my DNA bloodlines and Ancestral lines, all shame, guilt, and torture, including all the negative aspects of their actions into Luminous Light and Unconditional Love.

I bear witness today, and acknowledge the shortcomings, negative attitudes and beliefs, and I release into your Eternal Source, with the vibration of Christ-consciousness, all the negativity from all the generations that came before me, as I now integrate, perfect and restore the generational lines to the original beauty that they were always meant to be and represent.

Using the words of power: Arom Nahrea - Keli, Lekab, Lehah, Sael, Vaho, Doni, Aumem, Mabeh, Aiau - Arom Nahrea.

I command:

- My full DNA Identity record activation.
- Activation of my organic DNA codings.
- Activation of my WITCH DNA including all my spiritual gifts and powers.
- Alignment of the cosmic sovereign law and Krystal spiral flows of unity intelligence

- Activation of my Human 12 Tree Grid – the tree of life.
- Opening of the Crystalline seals and activation of my dormant DNA.
- Raise in vibration into the new Bliss Blueprint.
- Full energy, clarity, and body alignment.
- Strengthening of neurological circuitry to hold more light.
- Opening of more channels for higher self-embodiment.
- Activation of my heart-mind connection.
- Activation of the Sophianic body.
- Activation of the sacred Merkabah source energy and star.
- Activation of the ascension vehicle.
- Full embodiment of the avatar Christ body and monad oversoul.
- Activation of unity consciousness.

I now command the full reconnection of my sound and light bodies, activation of the diamond grid and 144 harmonics for full restoration and unification of the male and female energies within my planetary body.

I now choose to live in alignment with the universal laws embodying my true Divine essence, to live in abundance, health, joy and oneness and sovereignty from this time forwards.

And so, it is.

Thank you, thank you, thank you Divine. Thank you for this blessing".

Take some deep breaths – as you breathe in feel your heart fill with unconditional love and as you breathe out feel all heaviness or tension release from your body.

THE HEART-MIND CONNECT - THE MARRIAGE OF THE DIVINE FEMININE AND DIVINE MASCULINE

Now take some deep breaths before you start, just centring your energy, and as you exhale let go of any tension, stress or negative thoughts or emotions that are lingering.

Imagine, feel, or perceive a brilliant white light now streaming down through the top of your head (your crown chakra) and this luscious liquid light is now filling your entire body with pure white light. Your body and soul are now beaming with unconditional love and abundance!

Please read this out loud:

"Dearest Divine,

I request the blessing of Divine Light and manifestations of eternal love from every vibration of the Cosmic Mind to now assist me to activate my heart mind connection, bringing my Divine Feminine and Divine Masculine into unity and harmony now.

I command the full removal of:

- The Seven Houses of Ego.

- All Victim-victimizer programs.

- All negative beliefs, cords, contracts, curses, or conditions blocking the reconnection of the heart-mind.

- All 2D walls of separation of guilt, shame, unworthiness, self-doubt, lack of trust, betrayal, abandonment, anger, rage, fear, entrapment, and enslavement.

- All cellular memory of trauma or abuse.

- All predator forces and negative energies or entities.

- Blockages in the Pericardium Shield.

To allow the activation and purification of my heart-mind connection by unlocking the words of power: Arom Nahrea - Keli, Lekab, Lehah, Sael, Vaho, Doni, Aumem, Mabeh, Aiau - Arom Nahrea.

I now command full activation of:

- My heart-brain complex.

- The Crystal Heart.

- My Human 12 Tree Grid – the tree of life.

- Harmony and balance between my Divine Feminine and Divine Masculine.

- My 12 DNA strands and Aurora Body.

- Self-Compassion and Kindness. "

Now focus your attention on your heart space. Pull your awareness into this space. And as you do so, visualize, sense, or perceive a golden cord coming from this heart space. At the end of the cord is a plug and you see this cord now travel up towards your mind (your third eye chakra) and watch as this plug connects into this space and forms a circuit of continuous glowing, loving energy flowing in harmony between your heart and your mind.

Your mind feels clear and you feel deeply connected, peaceful, serene, and calm.

Your heart and mind are relaying messages of love and connection and you feel a wave of relief and calmness washing over your entire body. It is now safe for your heart and soul to be heard, witnessed, respected, and honoured by your mind.

This feels like a coming home for your soul and you feel powerful as your energy is aligned and in flow.

You surrender fully into this feeling and as you do you say out loud:

"I now anchor lock and seal this heart mind connection throughout my hologram, anchor lock and seal through my subconscious, my DNA and the time matrix.

And so, it is.

Thank you, thank you, thank you Divine".

CLEARING THE EMOTIONAL PAY OFF TO SELF-SABOTAGE

Now take some deep breaths before you start, just centring your energy, and as you exhale let go of any tension, stress or negative thoughts or emotions that are lingering.

Imagine, feel, or perceive a brilliant white light now streaming down through the top of your head (your crown chakra) and this luscious liquid light is now filling your entire body with pure white light. This light will assist you in releasing these old behaviours and patterns and dissolve them into liquid light.

Please read aloud with intention:

"Dearest Divine Loving Source,

Please bless me with your Divine Grace and assist me to safely release all self-sabotage behaviours and emotional payoffs so I may let go of and release, clear, dissolve and disconnect all negative attachments, cords, ties and connections to these behaviours."

Focus again on this luscious liquid light that is flowing down through your crown chakra and see yourself completely bathed in this light as it enters ever cell of your body.

As you stand in this light you witness the reasons for your self-sabotaging behaviour, and you realize that these behaviours are no longer necessary. You choose to let them go and forgive yourself. You send love to yourself and choose now to move forward leaving behind these negative emotions and behaviours.

You feel the healing light now moving through every cell of your being as your DNA is being upgraded and purified and reprogrammed with strength, courage and loving life force energy.

Connect with your Divine essence now and the feeling of love and acceptance as you choose to embrace all that you are.

Say aloud:

"I am free of these self-sabotaging behaviours and the need to keep playing small, I accept my gifts and step into my full power. I love the woman I am and the woman I am becoming.

Thank you, thank you, thank you.

And so, it is".

BELIEF REPROGRAMMING

Before you begin, if you have not already, open your sacred space and ensure you are somewhere you will not be disturbed. Make sure you are comfortable, take a few deep breaths as you centre your energy into your heart space as you connect within.

Say aloud:

"I call upon my Divine Loving Source, my spiritual evolution team, and all enlightened beings of love and above, to now assist me to reprogram my DNA.

I command access to Creator of All's Pure Divine Healing energy for support, access to all levels of advanced consciousness, dimensions and timelines now to remove and cancel the negative belief pattern of (list the negative belief) running in my master program in my subconscious mind and DNA".

Sensing brilliant white, cleansing, and healing light now encasing your entire being as it streams down through your crown chakra. The light is now drawing out this negative belief program and pattern from your entire energy system. Your spiritual team and angels are there to give you the healing that you need. You can feel this old negative program, including any fear, denial or stress associated with the program being dissolved in the light. Your body and energy system feels lighter and you feel the burden being lifted from you now.

New signals of love, happiness and joy are being created for you to download the new program and positive belief.

Say aloud:

"I now activate the new positive belief and program… (insert the positive program from the opposite side of the old belief) and anchor lock and seal this new program throughout my hologram, anchor lock and seal through my subconscious, my DNA and the time matrix.

I now activate the power sources of the 10 Attributes of God and the Universal Tree of Life throughout my entire energy system.

With gratitude, I confirm the upgrade of my master program.

And so it is".

NEGATIVE ENERGY REVERSAL

Say aloud:

"I call upon the Great Beloved, The Creator of All that is, and my spiritual evolution team to assist me now to clear and transmute all psychic attack energies, cords and attachments, negative energies and, negative thoughtforms directed towards me from (the name of the person who sent them).

I now sever and release all energetic cords that do not serve my highest good.

I release myself from these cords and ties across all dimensions, within all space and realities and throughout all frameworks of my existence, never to return again.

Please purify, cleanse, and restore my energy field releasing any negative impacts or after affects. Restore and activate my soul life force energy and realign me, mind-body-spirit to balance and harmonize my frequency.

I now seal myself with white and gold purifying light, and I send white light of love and blessings to whom it came from.

Thank you, thank you, thank you.

And so, it is".

CURSE REMOVAL

Before you begin, if you have not already, open your sacred space and ensure you are somewhere you will not be disturbed.

Say aloud:

"I call upon the Great Beloved, The Creator of All that is, and my spiritual evolution team and I ask that the highest vibrations of love and light connect with my highest self now to assist me to break the curse including all cords and attachments, negative energies and, negative thoughtforms directed towards me from (the name of the person who sent them).

I now sever, release, and dissolve all curses across all dimensions, within all space and realities and throughout all frameworks of my existence, never to return again.

I command purification and cleansing to restore my energy field releasing all negative impacts and after affects.

I request full activation of my power sources through the 10 emanations of the Tree of Life and I now seal myself with white and gold purifying light.

I send white light of love and blessings to whom the curse came from.

Thank you, thank you, thank you.

And so, it is".

KARMA REPAIR

Before you begin, if you have not already, open your sacred space and ensure you are somewhere you will not be disturbed.

Say aloud with intention:

"I call upon the powers of The Creator of All that is, the Lords of Karma, and my spiritual evolution team to assist in the cleansing, clearing and transmutation of all negative Karmic imprints in my Akasha.

I call on the Law of Forgiveness. I forgive everyone and everything and I ask forgiveness from everyone and everything. I forgive myself.

I ask to be surrounded with Divine purifying light and call upon the assistance of my protections angels to cleanse my energy on every level.

Dearest Divine, please release from my energy field, all that no longer serves me for my best and highest good, release it into the light and replace it with gratitude, compassion, and joy.

Step me into alignment with my highest Divine Truth.

I request full activation of my power sources through the 10 emanations of the Tree of Life and I now seal myself with white and gold purifying light.

Thank you, thank you, thank you.

And so, it is".

CONNECT ME ABOVE, BELOW AND WITHIN.

Say the following out loud with intention and passion:

"Dear Divine Loving Creator,

Please awaken the awareness within me now that I am worthy of love, abundance, joy, alignment, ease and flow in my life as I now surrender all resistance, all blocks, belief systems, all frequencies less than love from my energy system that are stopping me from embracing my birthright of sovereignty, peace and abundance.

I release them into Mother Earth for transmutation and transformation.

Please assist me to love myself unconditionally now.

With gratitude in my heart I welcome in, receive, and accept your infinite love, wisdom, and guidance.

I open my heart and my hands to willingly receive all the infinite abundance you offer to me.

I follow my heart always, as she knows the way. And following my heart's direction I take inspired action daily to align me to the all loving frequency of my divinity.

And so, it is.

Thank you, thank you, thank you Divine"

CHAKRA BALANCE AND ACTIVATION

This clearing and balancing of all your chakras, will bring you closer to yourself and bring a deeper connection with your Divine loving source, clearing the chakras for your chi energy to flow.

Say aloud:

"Dear Divine Loving Source,

Please allow me to release any energies or frequencies less than love now, so I may fully activate and balance my chakras deepening my connection with you and my inner guidance".

Closing your eyes take another deep breath in, allowing yourself to be here. Allow yourself to take in this moment to be who you really are. This moment in time is an important one allowing you to remember who you truly are.

Beyond the external influences in your life, allow yourself to tap into the deep reservoir that is your authentic self.

First become aware of your breath.

Breathing deeply in and as you do breathe in beautiful unconditional love and as you breathe out letting go of all stress and worries. Get comfortable and know there is no other place you need to be.

Allow yourself to drop into a space where you feel safe, a space where you feel love,

Now see white light fill every single cell of your being streaming down into your crown chakra on the top of your head. gently moving through all the way to your toes.

Take another deep breath and as you exhale feel your whole body surrendering and relaxing. Allow any thoughts to simply drift away or place them in a box to deal with later. Allow any sounds you hear to become a part of this meditation.

Give yourself permission to experience this meditation knowing that whatever you experience is in perfect order and harmony with your destiny.

You are now surrounded by your Angels and Spirit Guides.

You hear yourself say "Angels and Guides please surround me now".

You feel safe and peaceful.

Now imagine, see, or perceive that you have a light above your head. This light signifies the essence of the Divine loving source. You feel safe and protected with this light. Allow the light to be any colour that comes to you. It is perfect. If the light changes colour at any time, allow that too. Everything is just as it should be.

Know that you are receiving exactly what you need from the Divine source and your higher self. Trust this process.

You are bathed in this beautiful light. You can feel it on your skin and surrounding your whole body.

Imagine this light now enters the top of your head, your Crown Chakra.

The Crown Chakra is associated with the colour purple.

You allow the light to enter. You can feel any blocks that are blocking the top of your head, melt away with ease. You feel the light opening the top of your head like a flower blossoming. It fills any emptiness you have there.

You hear yourself say, "I now allow the Divine Loving Source to enter me and clarify my thoughts".

You feel a connection to the Source of All. And you feel this light switching on your Claircognisence (this is your knowing).

Pay attention now to the spot between your eyes, your Third Eye. The Third Eye Chakra is associated with the colour indigo or dark blue.

You notice whether your Third Eye is open or closed. The light clears away any blocks inside your head and in front of your Third Eye.

You hear yourself say "I now allow my Spiritual vision to manifest clearly".

You feel your natural Clairvoyance switch on. See your Third Eye open and see this light now entering and filling the area and streaming out of your Third Eye.

The light also clears blocks inside your head where your Ear Chakra is. The Ear Chakra is associated with the colour magenta.

You hear yourself say, "I now allow myself to hear Spirit clearly". Feel your Clairaudience switch on and your Spiritual Ears clear and become receptive.

The light travels down to your throat, clearing a space there so it is easier to breath and speak your truth. The Throat Chakra is associated with the colour light blue.

Feel this light expand your Throat Chakra. Feel any blocks being removed that prevent you from speaking your truth.

You hear yourself say, "I now allow myself to speak my truth with integrity".

The light transforms and expands your Throat Chakra. Notice yourself feeling the courage and wisdom to speak up for yourself and what you believe in.

The light moves down to your heart. The Heart Chakra is associated with the colour green. Notice any blocks and emptiness in different areas in your heart. Feeling the light melting away all blocks and filling any emptiness.

You hear yourself say, "I now allow Divine loving source to fill and open my heart".

Feel your Intuition and Clairsentience switch on. Feel the light expanding your heart Chakra through the front and the back. Feel yourself more connected to all beings. Feeling more compassion.

Feeling safe to allow your heart to open. Knowing this is a gift you give to yourself. Notice this softening and expansive feeling fill your heart. It is safe to love and be loved now.

Feeling this light traveling down now to your solar plexus. The place between your heart and stomach. The Solar Plexus Chakra is associated with the colour yellow. This centre of your being is now filled with this loving light. See any blocks or toxins being dissolved by the light.

You hear yourself say, "I now allow myself to feel powerful". Feeling your self-esteem increase as you feel one with Divine source. Knowing that you indeed are a manifestation of this source. Knowing that you are worthy of embracing the essence of the Divine.

That this is who you are. You are connected to Divine Source in a profound way. You know that as you say yes to the very source from which you are created, so too will you manifest unlimited abundance in your life.

Now the light travels down to your stomach, your Sacral Chakra. The Sacral Chakra is associated with the colour orange. You notice any emptiness replaced and refuelled by Divine loving source. You notice any blocks or toxic waste is being removed.

And You hear yourself say "I now allow myself to feel whole, joyful and complete".

You feel full and peaceful at the same time. The only permanent thing that can fill you here is source energy. All other attachments are temporal and unnecessary. Feel yourself embrace this light with enthusiasm. Feel the joy and certainty of contentment filling your entire body as you accept this Divine source into your stomach.

The light now travels down to your Base Chakra. The Base Chakra is associated with the colour red.

You notice this light fills your base Chakra, the sexual organs and transforms any blocks or emptiness into a completely safe and nurturing feeling.

You hear yourself say, "I now allow myself to completely trust". Feel how it feels to allow Divine Source to be fully housed in your temple.

Feel this light traveling down to your feet. Imagine that your feet have roots at the bottom of them. Feel these roots go down deep into the centre of the Earth. Feel yourself one with the Earth. You are now grounded. Completely grounded whilst being connected to Spirit.

Feel yourself clear and filled with the Spiritual light of Divine loving source through your whole body.

From your Crown Chakra down to your Base Chakra. Feel the light surround you now. You feel the light within your body, throughout the front and back of your body and all around you.

You are filled and surrounded by the Source of All. You are connected above, below, and all around you. Enjoy this feeling and know that this feeling is your birthright.

Feel a celebration now from the Angels and Guides all around you. You are deeply connected; you feel aligned and full of Divine loving energy.

Thank you, thank you, thank you Divine.

As you count to 3 come back into fully waking consciousness remembering this experience and committing to the practice of clearing and connecting daily.

1, 2, 3.

Say aloud:

"I now choose to maintain a continuous and clear connection of energy flowing throughout my energy system. I claim my birthright of connection to the Creator of All that is, to my Divine loving source. It is my gift to be and live in my fullest power.

And so, it is".

SELF-WORTH AND SELF-LOVE ACTIVATION

Take a deep breath, get comfortable. Nothing else matters right now but your own personal breakthrough, your own gift to yourself.

Place your hands over your heart chakra and bring all your awareness to your body. Feel your body. Relax into your body. Feel your breath, breathing in unconditional love and feel this love as it spreads throughout your mind and your muscles, from your head to your toes.

Enjoy the feeling of lightness, enjoy the feeling of being calm and relaxed.

Take a deeper breath. Breathing in and out rhythmically.

Drop into the space within, a space where you feel safe, a space where you feel peace, a space where you feel love, allowing the worries of the world around you to fall away, to fall off the left side of your body and off the right side of your body.

Your whole energy is you, vibrating and slowing into a beautiful state of comfort.

Say aloud:

"Dearest Divine Creator of All,

Please allow me to release any frequency less than love now. I release all feelings and doubts of worth to you now, all negative thoughts and emotions that do not serve my highest good, I release them to you for transmutation and transformation.

I now call upon the blessings of your Divine Grace to activate a deep self-love and compassion throughout my emotional, physical, mental, and spiritual bodies, my DNA, and my subconscious mind, throughout all timelines and frameworks of my existence.

Please restore my DNA to my original Divine Bliss Blueprint so I am reconnected to Unity Consciousness.

Thank you Thank you Thank you Divine. Thank you for blessing me.

And so, it is".

POWERFUL ENERGETIC CORD CUTTING RELEASE

Now take some deep breaths before you start, just centring your energy, and as you exhale let go of any tension, stress or negative thoughts or emotions that are lingering.

Imagine, feel, or perceive a brilliant white light now streaming down through the top of your head (your crown chakra) and this luscious liquid light is now filling your entire body with pure white light.

Say aloud with intention:

"Dearest Divine Loving Source,

I call upon your powers of Divine light, blessings and protection to heal, let go, and cut any etheric cords that are no longer serving my best and highest good.

I request that all cords attaching and binding me and (name of the person you wish to cut ties and cords with) that are not aligned with the frequency of love, light and abundance now be released.

I now sever and release all energetic cords that do not serve my highest good.

I release myself from these binds, contracts, cords and ties and I confirm that all cords and ties are now destroyed across all dimensions, within all space and realities and throughout all frameworks of my existence, never to return again.

I hereby banish these energetic cords and recover now all energy that was harvested or siphoned from my soul or my life force energy.

I confirm the full release of any and all negative after affects or repercussions from this karmic release now.

I send love, light and blessings to myself and (the name of person cords/attachments were with) and seal myself in a protective violet circle filled with brilliant, shimmering, purifying, Divine light.

Take some deep breaths and feel your energy now flowing back to you, filling you once again with vitality and creating a peaceful energetic boundary of love and light.

Thank you thank you thank you Divine.

And so, it is".

SOUL MATE ATTRACTION ACTIVATION

Say aloud with passion and intention:

"Dear Divine Loving Source, the Creator of All that is,

I ask for assistance from all beings of love and higher, the ascended masters, the Lords of Karma, enlightened beings and guardians, my spiritual evolution team, and the full co-operation of my higher self for the soulmate attraction activation.

I hereby banish, release, sever and delete all cords of attachment, all contracts, belief systems and all unresolved karma between myself and all my previous partners for my best and highest good.

I confirm all blocks to my most compatible soulmate in this lifetime have now been removed, cancelled, cleared, deleted, and erased in all directions of time, never to return.

I now step into a new timeline where I now easily and gracefully attract love into my life.

I know and understand that I am worthy of great love and am entitled to all the beauty life has to offer me. Everywhere I look I see love, in every tree, flower, river and all of nature. I feel loved in all my forms now and I open my heart and welcome this love into my heart with joy.

I deeply love and appreciate myself. I am a unique being with amazing talents and I am confident in exactly who I am. I accept myself fully on every level now

My interactions with others reflect just how deeply I love and accept myself now.

I am regarded as valuable because I value myself. My mind is filled with loving thoughts for myself and others. I am a beautiful, confident, intelligent, powerful, loving and capable woman.

The qualities I desire in my soulmate connections are obvious to me now. I can see them written before me on a big screen within my mind."

- Visualise or perceive this list now forming in front of your eyes, in your mind's eye, on that big screen. Take some time to think of all the qualities you desire.

Say aloud:

"My soul mate is attracted to the values and qualities I possess, and I only attract those connections with those who possess the qualities I seek.

I am now surrounded by connections with others who are ready for a loving soulmate relationship commitment. Those that will give of themselves, spiritually, mentally, emotionally, and physically, freely, and easily.

I request that my energy field be cleansed, strengthened, and upgraded so I now attract unconditional love to myself like a magnet".

-All your energy now floods back to you, filling you with brilliant white light.

See this light now swirl around you in a rapid clockwise spiral and then return to your energy field, giving you a boost of vitality and surrounding you in a sphere of white protective light.

You are now open to love. You know what you want, and your soulmate can see you as clearly as you see them now. You welcome love into your life each day. You have a deep love for yourself and in doing so, you welcome others to love and be loved by you.

Say aloud:

"I, (your name) confirm that all blocks, cords and attachments to previous relationships have now been dissolved with love and gratitude. I am now ready to connect fully with my true Divine soulmate and I choose this for myself now

And so, it is. Thank you, thank you, thank you Divine".

MONEY AND ABUNDANCE AFFIRMATION ACTIVATION

Recite daily out loud:

"Dearest Divine Creator,

Please let me release any frequency less than love now. Allow me to let go of all negative thoughts, feelings and beliefs around money and abundance and open my eyes so I may see and know the truth that sets me free.

I release all cell memories stopping me from receiving abundance in my life now

I share the Divine nature. I love and accept all that I am.

My energy is my currency and I am aligned with the frequency of wealth and abundance.

- I am a magnet for money.
- My wealth shines from within me.
- I allow myself to be drenched with financial abundance always, and I generously share my wealth.
- I radiate wealth, abundance, and prosperity.
- My riches are forever increasing as I give more of myself in service to the world.
- My body, mind and soul are beaming with love and abundance.

And so, it is.

Thank you, thank you, thank you".

POVERTY CONSCIOUSNESS CLEARING AND FULL RESTORATION OF THE ORIGINAL CRYSTALLINE BLUEPRINT

Before you begin, if you have not already, open your sacred space and ensure you are somewhere you will not be disturbed. As always, free to light some candles, play soft, soothing music, hold or place crystals around you, whatever feels right, allow yourself to be guided by your own intuition.

"Dear Divine Loving Source, the Creator of All that is,

I request assistance from all enlightened beings of love and higher, the ascended masters, my spiritual evolution team, and the full co-operation of my higher self.

I command the full erasure of:

All poverty consciousness frequencies,
All Egyptian black magic and money curses,
All debt and enslavement programs,
All Power Elite and Cabal control structures,
All addiction, mind control, and materialism programs and false karma,

including all fear-based propaganda and engineering that has been programmed in my DNA, my subconscious mind and archetypal body.

I now download and install my original Divine creation blueprint into my DNA, subconscious mind, and archetypal body of:

Unconditional Love,
Creation,
Abundance,
Joy,
Gratitude,
Freedom, and Oneness.

I now call for full restoration of my 617 living soul facets including full harmonizing of each of the five individual sections therein:

The Word,
The Actus,
The Prima,
The Nomen,

The Spiritual Name.

Activating the words of power,

Arom Nahrea -
Keli,
Lekab,
Lehah,
Sael,
Vaho,
Doni,
Aumem,
Mabeh,
Aiau
- Arom Nahrea.

I now call in, accept, and receive all the blessings of good fortune, prosperity and abundance offered to me from my esteemed spiritual guides, goddesses, angels and deities. Thank you, thank you, thank you. I now request to connect with love coded hydroplasmic light and activate in my human body, the Silicate Matrix DNA template - the original human crystalline blueprint

I am now completely aligned to my original Divine blueprint of abundance.

And so it is"

WEALTH AND ABUNDANCE ACTIVATION

Repeat aloud:

"Dear Divine Loving source please allow me to release all energies and frequencies less than love with ease and grace now. I release all struggle and surrender fully to release all blocks, belief systems and fear in the way of me embracing my birthright of Divine abundance.

I hereby release all the pain, fear and conditioning that has made me feel small and unworthy of financial abundance.

Help me to forgive myself and all others who may have previously made me feel insecure or undeserving of my power and my ability to manifest, receive and accept abundance and money.

I allow my consciousness to shift as I gracefully step into knowing and feeling I deserve love, abundance, wealth, and joy in my life consistently now".

Take a deep breath in then release allowing yourself to get comfortable. Closing your eyes take another deep breath in, allowing yourself to be here. Allow yourself to take in this moment to be who you really are.

This moment in time is an important one allowing you to remember who you truly are beyond the external influences in your life, allow yourself to tap into the deep reservoir that is your authentic self.

First become aware of your breath. Breathing deeply in and as you do, breathing in beautiful unconditional love and as you breathe out letting go of all stress, tension, worry and fear. Get comfortable and know there is no other place you need to be. Allow yourself to drop into a space where you feel safe, a space where you feel love.

Visualise white light filling every single cell of your being streaming down into your crown chakra on the top of your head and gently moving through all the way to your toes. This brilliant white light is clearing and aligning all the chakras throughout your entire body.

Feel this beam of light cleansing and clearing all the stagnant energy that no longer serves you as you feel yourself becoming energetically aligned. Surrender to this warm energy radiating through your whole body. Now quiet your mind and simply relax. Release any resistance.

Repeat aloud:

"Creator of All,

I am ready to be surrounded by experiences that nurture and support me and allow me to fully expand into the truest version of my soul. I trust and I surrender knowing that you are my faithful guide. Please bless me with the same trust and faith in myself.

I now choose and align to receiving an abundance of money doing what I love, my passion, as I embrace my energy as my currency.

I put myself first now, I take care of my health and in doing so I am able to help those I love.

I communicate with strength and clarity and this is expressed in my words and actions now.

My energy is harmonious, consistent, and strong. I am the master of my emotions and my intuition and I am powerful and successful. I have complete trust in myself and the incredible life I am creating filled with love, abundance, flow and ease.

I am sure of myself; secure. I am confident and powerful and any old desperation, fear, lack or need to make my life happen right now is renewed with a sense of calmness and peace.

Every cell of my body sparkles with the energy of love, clarity, and power.

I honour and trust myself.

Even though I do not definitively know the path to the future, I honour and trust the path I am taking will lead me to my best future. A future of love, abundance, and success in my life.

I take inspired action; I follow my intuition, and this fills my heart and soul with such joy. I listen to my soul, connect with my heart and this moves me into a deep trust and flow and as I focus intently on my heart's desires this powerfully magnetizes abundance into my life.

I welcome in, receive, and graciously accept a continual flow of money consistently with ease and flow now, as I shift from fear into love, the financial miracles continue to flow in. I gracefully and gratefully accept this as my normal now.

I declare, I no longer sacrifice my desires, dreams, wishes, or needs. I am a powerful manifestor and the master creator of my life. I am abundant and aligned with the frequency of abundance. I continuously and consistently create abundance with ease, grace and flow.

I am a money magnet.

Money flows into my life easily and is attracted to my energy.

I am a miracle and I attract miracles in my life consistently.

I am aligned with the energy of money.

My energy is my currency."

Place your hands over your heart and your solar plexus chakras and imagine, sense, or perceive sending loving energy to these areas. You are opening your heart and activating your soul's wealth energy prosperity.

You are a wealthy, loving, talented and powerful woman. And you love the woman you are and the woman you are becoming.

Thank you, thank you, thank you for rising up and thriving.

And so, it is"

ALIGN, UPGRADE AND BALANCE THE ENERGY SYSTEM

Say aloud:

"Dearest Divine,

I request access to the powerful Universal Blue Star Light frequencies to balance, realign and activate my entire Chakra and Nadial system to reconnect, align and attune my physical and spiritual bodies. I release any negative or obsolete subtle energies, and any frequency less than love now.

I request full upgrade of my Nadial structure, my angelic human 12 Strand DNA silicate matrix and my original Diamond Sun blueprint".

Bring your focus in now to your breath and visualize or perceive a beautiful sphere of Blue Star Light now connecting with your breath, moving throughout your body and filling you with this healing light with every breath you take.

Breathing into the heart space, bring your awareness here now.

Continue to breathe deeper while focused on the centre of your heart.

Take a deeper breath in and on the exhale intend to push your breath downward, pushing your breath down the centre of your body and into your pelvis, and pushing your exhaling breath further down and outward for a complete release.

Repeat this exhaling downward breath pattern three times.

Say aloud:

"With gratitude I accept the full reconnection and activation of my energy body.

Thank you, thank you, thank you.

And so, it is".

PHYSICAL UPGRADE

Say aloud:

"Dear Creator of All that is,

Please assist me to release all toxins including all vaccine toxins, physical and emotional traumas, disease, allergies, dehydration, inflammation, and any and all nutritional deficiencies from my physical body. I now choose to release all physical pain associated with past life deaths or torture, and all cell memories affecting my body. I release all causes of my physical misalignment, through all timelines, throughout all space and realities and all frameworks of my existence.

I request my physical body be reconnected, aligned, attuned, and all my DNA now be upgraded and recalibrated to my original Divine blueprint. I choose sovereignty from this moment forwards.

Thank you, thank you, thank you.

And so it is".

EMOTIONAL RELEASE

1. Fear	2. Guilt	3. Shame	4. Anger
5. Resentment	6. Unappreciated	7. Sacrificed	8. Hurt
9. Unworthy	10. Depressed	11. Grief	12. Abandoned
13. Jealous	14. Inadequate	15. Foolish	16. Desperate
17. Anxious	18. Weepy	19. Nervous	20. Resistance

Use muscle testing to determine which emotions need to be released.

Once you have your list of emotions, use the following command to release them.

Say aloud:

"Dearest Divine,

I call upon your Divine grace and blessings to assist me to release the following emotions.

(List emotions)

With love, blessings and gratitude for the lessons, wisdom and understanding these experiences and emotions have served.

I now choose to clear and transmute these emotions into spiritual compost and send them back to Mother Earth to be alchemized into unconditional love.

Thank you, thank you, thank you.

And so, it is".

Take a few deep breaths and release all the residue down through your base chakra and into Mother Earth.

ACTIVATING THE SPIRITUAL BODY - TREE OF LIFE ACTIVATION

Say aloud:

"I call for the assistance of The Creator of All, my spiritual evolution team, and my higher self to activate and awaken my full spiritual body.

I command the full removal of the false matrix and all global control systems to enable the activation and reconnection of the 44 DNA codes containing the records of all that I am.

I request activation of the double-helix, two strands of physical DNA, determining the characteristics of my physical body and the 10 strands of etheric DNA containing the entire history of my soul, my spiritual essence, and the truth of who I really am.

Activating the words of power:

Arom Nahrea -
Keli,
Lekab,
Lehah,
Sael,
Vaho,
Doni,
Aumem,
Mabeh,
Aiau
- Arom Nahrea.

I now access Pure Divine Universal Source energy to activate the 12 layers of my DNA.

Layer 1: The Tree of Life - the courage to move ahead and integrate my fears.

Layer 2: The Blueprint of Life – the ability to focus on something and follow it to completion.

Layer 3: The Present Consciousness Awakening - maintaining gender balance between male and female power.

Layer 4: The Belief Layer - balance between my energy field and physical body.

Layer 5: The Awakening Self– the ability to live peacefully in a state of acceptance.

Layer 6: The I Am That I Am Layer (this is the most sacred and Divine layer) – the strength to stand in my truth regardless of the outcome.

Layer 7: The Balance Layer– the ability to accept both my dark and light sides.

Layer 8: The Truth Layer – the ability to hold personal boundaries regardless of outcomes.

Layer 9: Opening the Blind Eye (or Seeing without Illusion) – the ability to accept and live within a diverse community.

Layer 10: Remembrance – the ability to tune into and listen to my soul, my higher-self.

Layer 11: Realization – the power to envision, create and manifest my visions in 3D.

Layer 12: God (or the Creator) – the ability to be accepting, kind, and appreciate the value in all things.

I now align my energy with the Cosmic Trinity and confirm my sovereignty to the benevolent universal and galactic matrix.

Thank you, thank you, thank you.

And so, it is".

NEW MOON BLESSINGS RITUAL

WHAT DO YOU WANT TO ACHIEVE? *What is the new goal that you wish to attain?*

Is there something that you keep thinking about? Are you fulfilling your passion? Are you listening to your intuition? Is there something that you can accomplish this month that could change your life for the better? This goal can be personal, professional, or any kind of goal that you want! Write down as many ideas as you like!

EMBODIMENT. *What new routine do you wish to embody to help you with your goals?*

Implementing a healthy habit will ensure that you stick to your goal above. What kind of lifestyle changes can you make to help make your dream goal a reality?

AWAKENING NEW SKILLS AND GIFTS. *What new qualities do you wish to encourage?*

This could be anything from learning a new technique such as cooking or gardening to being a good listener, or even writing letters to far away friends. Pick something different that you do not normally that could add value to your life.

IT'S MY LIFE. *What kind of life do you wish to lead?*

When envisioning your future life, it is important to not only see it but feel what it would be like. What would your ideal life feel like? And what do you need to do to get there?

THE ATTITUDE OF GRATITUDE. *What are you grateful for?*

Gratitude attracts more gratitude and the more that you praise your current winnings, the more you will attract things to be grateful for. Choose 5 things (big or small), that make you smile.

Once done with your wishes write them down as a list of wishes you want to call in with the new moon. Make 2 copies. One to be saved and one to be burned.

Take time to prepare yourself for your ritual, play some music, burn candles, oils, sage or anything that evokes meaning for you.

Recite your wishes as if already your blessings, ask to be blessed with the ability to create these things in your 3D reality.

Burn one copy under the New Moon and take some time to feel into what these blessings would mean for you. Keep the other copy in a safe space or under your pillow or in your nightstand to recite regularly and bring your wishes into reality.

WITCH tip:

An example of how to write your list of wishes.

NEW MOON PLEASE BLESS ME WITH:

_____

_____

_____

_____

_____

_____

_____

_____

_____

_____

_____

_____

_____

_____

_____

And feel free to use bright colour or glitter pens that will shimmer in the moonlight!

Afterword

A huge thank you for making it this far. There is a lot here to take in, so break it down into digestible pieces and revisit it often.

I wanted to provide true value to you with a book that not only talks to you but will grow with you.

This guide will become your best friend.

You will create miracles in your life as you follow each and every chapter, and it won't stop there.

Each time you use one of the invocations or activations, you will be activating your DNA and your WITCH gifts on a deeper and deeper level as you harness the power that lives within you.

I thank your spirit for leading you here and bless you with an abundance of love and Magick!

Bless you beautiful Divine woman, Bless you.

Karen xo

WITCH

www.ingramcontent.com/pod-product-compliance
Lightning Source LLC
Chambersburg PA
CBHW050304010526
44107CB00055B/2098